ACHIEVING MINDFULNESS THROUGH ASTROLOGY

using the energy of the signs
to increase your wellbeing

Karen Marsh

CONTENTS

Title Page

Copyright

Foreword by Donna Maxine

Introduction

Why Do We Need to Be Mindful?   1

The Astrology Signs   3

How to Approach Being Mindful   42

The Benefits of Mindfulness   49

Why Is Mindfulness So Effective?   54

The Three Paths to Mindfulness   58

The Paradoxes of Mindfulness   168

Making Mindfulness a Habit   172

How Astrology Signs Deal with Stress   175

Mindfulness as Part of Your Life   191

References and Further Study   193

FOREWORD BY
DONNA MAXINE

I have been lucky enough to have astrological guidance from Karen Marsh for nearly 40 years - she is my sister!

We're living in unprecedented times at the moment and we need to do all we can to keep ourselves centred! Mindfulness has gained massive popularity over the last few years and can be a very effective 'tool' for us to use to help us stay calm. However, because we are all different, a mindfulness practice that works for one person doesn't necessarily work for someone else.

Understanding our inner strengths and weaknesses, revealed by our Zodiac sign and personal astrology, is helpful at the best of times - but especially now. In this book, Karen combines her vast astrological knowledge and her understanding of mindfulness techniques to guide us to the best way of coping with these changing times. This will help us gain a deeper awareness of which mindfulness techniques work for YOU depending on your star sign. Tailoring information to our specific star sign and personal astrological traits, Karen has practical and helpful advice for everyone, even if we have no previous knowledge of Astrology.

This is an enlightening book which can also give us insight into helping ourselves, or the people close to us, attain inner peace in the best way depending on our individual astrological needs. This can be especially helpful (to keep in mind) for our children and teenagers.

Even if you have found that you haven't been able to 'master' the practice of mindfulness before, reading this book should make it much easier for you, as the advice Karen shares is both illuminating and simple to apply in daily life.

Donna Maxine
August 2020

INTRODUCTION

*Mindfulness isn't difficult. We just need
to remember to do it ~ Sharon Saltzberg*

Mindfulness (and being mindful) is becoming increasingly important in our hectic modern society. As more and more research is being done on the benefits of mindfulness and how it is linked to happiness and wellbeing, more of us are trying to incorporate these practices into our everyday life. But what does mindfulness actually mean? What do you need to do to achieve mindfulness? And why do some people seem to find it easier than others?

Mindfulness just means giving something your undivided attention. Easy to say, but very hard to do! It occurs when your full attention is on what you are doing, or on what is happening, and you are not distracted. Another meaning of mindfulness is bringing yourself into the present moment, fully focusing on what is going on, just being an observer, not trying to control anything or make any judgements

So where does astrology come into all this? The stars and planets are always moving, and your natal chart (your astrology birth chart) shows a picture of the sky at the moment you were born. Where the planets are determines your temperament and personality and, in turn, your temperament and personality will determine how you approach being mindful.

Most people know where the Sun was in the sky when they were born because it is linked to the months of the year. The Sun is generally found in the same place in the sky at the same times each year because the Earth's orbit around the Sun is fairly constant. But there is more to consider in astrology than just your Sun sign (your astrology sign); other important influences are the overall balance of energy, the Ascendant (the sign rising on the eastern horizon at the time and place of birth) and the Moon sign. (Actually, all of the planets affect your personality, but these four are usually the most influential). These other astrological influences can't be found without casting a natal chart (or at least looking up a lot of data), but as the Sun sign is so important in your chart, just knowing that one thing will enable you to approach mindfulness practice in a new light. (Obviously, if you know other details of your chart, you can also apply those as well.)

Your Sun sign will be a big influence on how you practise mindfulness, but remember it isn't the only one. I therefore advise you to try anything you are drawn to in this book. Just because you are not that particular sign does not mean that it won't work for you; it may be that you have that sign emphasised in your chart and it will resonate with you regardless of where your Sun is. The specifics of how your Sun sign will influence your approach to mindfulness are scattered throughout the book.

I am writing this in the middle of the COVID-19 pandemic, and the whole world has now changed. We are all facing disruption in every aspect of our lives. We are having to deal with scaremongering by the media and with the uncertainty of what is going to happen, both now and in the future. In my opinion, there has never been a better time to learn how to calm and centre ourselves, how to manage our emotions and how to be happier in our lives. This is the time, more than any other, when it will benefit us all to learn how to be mindful.

WHY DO WE NEED TO BE MINDFUL?

It is the mark of an educated mind to be able to entertain a thought without accepting it ~ Aristotle

Before we look at how to practise mindfulness, it may be worth considering why we need to bother with it at all. There has been a lot of research and scientific study over the last few years looking at how to achieve happiness and wellbeing, and what makes one person happier than someone else. Most of this research concludes that the single most important thing for being happy is mindfulness. We, as humans, have this remarkable ability to let our minds stray from the present. You can be working at your computer and at the same time you could be thinking about your forthcoming holiday and what you're going to have for dinner and if you do really want to go out after work. This ability we have, that allows us to focus on things other than the present, is amazing.

It allows us to learn, plan and reason in ways that no other animal can.

However, this mind-wandering ability and happiness levels are connected. The latest research found that when people let their mind wander away from what they are doing, they are less happy. It actually doesn't matter what they were doing - even if it was something boring or difficult, they were happier if they focused their attention on it. It has been suggested that one of the reasons for this is that when our minds wander we often think about unpleasant things such as our worries, regrets and anxieties. Yet even if we are thinking about something neutral, or even pleasant, we are still less happy than if our mind isn't wandering at all. And we generally let our minds wander at least 50% of the time.

So, if we can find a way of not letting our minds wander, we would be happier. Of course, no one can stay focused on the present all of the time. Sometimes it's even good to let our minds wander, for example at the dentist or to plan a future event, but it is also good to have the ability to be mindful too, as this will increase our overall happiness levels.

It can be quite hard for us to achieve mindfulness, especially when we first start, so before we look into how to even begin to think about being mindful, we need to consider the astrology signs and how they can influence our approach to this.

THE ASTROLOGY SIGNS

Astrology is a language. If you understand the language, the sky speaks to you ~ Dane Rudhyar

Astrology is the study of the Sun, Moon and planets and their influence on the life and evolution of humanity. It influences the personality, behaviour and temperament of every individual, and studying the natal (birth) chart can reveal many things about the native (the person whose chart it is). The best-known aspect of modern astrology is the Zodiac and the twelve signs associated with it. The word 'Zodiac' is used to describe a band of sky that incorporates the twelve constellations of stars bearing the names of the signs, from Aries to Pisces. The Sun, Moon and planets sweep across this band of stars as they travel on their path through the heavens. These days, the twelve sections of the sky that have the names of the signs are fixed in place in the Zodiac and do not match up with the star constellations that have the same names. The heavens are continually moving, and this has caused the constellations (clusters of stars) and the twelve Zodiac signs (that we all know today) to move apart. Therefore, do not confuse the 'signs' with the constellations after which they are named.

Almost everyone knows the sign they were born under – their Sun sign, or star sign, because it is linked to the months of the year. The Sun is generally found in the same place in the sky at the same time each year because the Earth's orbit around the Sun is fairly constant. The actual day the Sun enters a new sign varies from 19th to 23rd of each month, but it gives you a general guide. If you were born on the dates when the signs could possibly change, then the only way to be certain where the Sun was at your birth is to have your horoscope cast.

But there is far more to astrology than just knowing your Sun sign. The sign you were born under is only one factor that must be considered in astrological interpretation. We must also consider: the signs that contain the Moon and the other planets, the sign crossing the eastern horizon at the time of birth (called the Ascendant), where they are positioned in the sky and their relationships to each other. Also, the overall energy of the chart is important.

Every horoscope contains the basic energy that comes from the Sun, Moon and planets, and you will always have this energy influencing you throughout your life. However, there are an infinite number of ways in which the planetary energies can be combined, as they are influenced by your environment and upbringing. Consequently, when looking at a birth chart we can only point out the possible abilities shown in it, any differences that may need to be resolved, and the conflicts (or areas of stress) that may need to be dealt with. The chart will identify any strengths and weaknesses that are in your character so that you can maximise your potential and make the most of your assets, but it will also show how you can deal with any vulnerabilities so they will no longer affect you.

You always have a choice about how you act in any situation and you can use any of the potential energy available to you, within the limits of your chart. You can achieve all of the possibilities shown in your chart, and you can also experience the conflicts as potential areas of stress. Linked to this, there are two main ways of working with, and understanding, the astrology signs. Each sign incorporates lessons, and, as these lessons are being learned, the talents and qualities of the signs develop. We will all feel (and express) most of the qualities that are shown by our sign, but we also need to remember that as well as developing the positive qualities, we must work with the more challenging traits and learn how to live with them and express them. For example, Aries is very impatient. This is a challenge; Aries natives need to learn how to manage and control this and must understand how to find strategies and techniques that enable them to remain calm in situations they usually find irritating. However, they also need to work on developing patience. (Controlling impatience and developing patience are not quite the same thing, although they are similar!) You may also find that you don't seem to show some of the qualities that are connected to your sign. Take Aries again: Arians are renowned to be natural leaders (deemed to be a 'positive' quality), but you may personally not like being in charge, or being a leader in any way, even though you are Aries. This means that one of your lessons is to develop your leadership skills.

All of the signs have characteristics which can be perceived as 'good' or 'bad'. There is no good or bad in astrology really, it is how we as individuals respond to the particular energies we experience that result in behaviours that we label good or bad. The descriptions of the signs that follow include lots of behaviour and personality traits and they may say things that you feel is a negative characteristic, or, alternatively, a positive one. Remember, though, the description is just the potential behaviour that may possibly manifest. Knowing the 'positive' and 'negative' elements of your sign will enable you to make the inner effort needed to balance conflicting elements, so that you will be able to build your life and character into a harmonious whole and so achieve the best that you can. We all need to develop all of the qualities of our sign, including those that we find difficult, and remembering this is important when we look at how to be mindful. The following descriptions of the signs is aimed at their potential approach to mindfulness - it is not a complete catalogue of their characteristics. It summarises the 'pure energy' of the sign, and no one is entirely one sign so no one is going to be identical to these descriptions. However, we will go into more detail about signs and mindfulness later on.

Aries

The Ram
21st March – 20th April

Aries is the Cardinal Fire sign. Cardinal signs like to start things and Fire signs are enthusiastic and passionate. You are therefore full of energy and enthusiasm and believe in the power of positive thinking and positive action. You hate being ill or in any way in a position of dependency and accepting your own human limitations and emotional needs is often difficult for you. (This is one of the lessons you need to learn). You love anything that presents you with a sense of adventure. Experiences that allow you to express yourself as a leader and use your natural ability to take the initiative especially appeal to you. You sometimes resent being told how to do something and you would rather have the freedom to do things your own way. You have executive and organising ability, which is mainly directed towards starting things – sustaining projects is not your strength, but initiating them is. Although you love to start something (you have all the ideas and plans, and you get everything in place) you will lose interest in it if progress is too slow or things have become too complicated or too boring. Ideas and creative projects seem to flow from you in a never-ending stream, but you often can't be bothered with the finer details of your plan; you prefer to see the big picture. You are not afraid of trying something that's never been done before and you always need to be busy, especially with your hands. You are a person who thrives on challenge (routine and sameness are boring!) but you may sometimes feel that you must battle your way through life, depending upon no one and nothing but your own strength, intelligence, and courage. You believe in being totally honest, true to yourself and your own vision and convictions, even if that means standing alone. Honesty, integrity, personal honour, and authenticity are important to you, and it can sometimes appear that you have little sympathy for weakness of character in others.

Because you are generally so enthusiastic about your projects or goals, you may inadvertently ignore other people's feelings and interests. This can make you appear a bit aggressive in your attitudes and you can sometimes struggle relating to others, in picking up subtle messages and nuances, listening, nurturing, and harmonising. You tend to get impatient if events don't move as quickly as you would like or if you just want to get on with things, and this can make you seem rather insensitive, and you sometimes push away others without meaning to. You have a mind of your own, and generally you do not care if anyone else agrees with you.

You like to be the first to do everything, and often you take risks that others consider unwise. Just be careful to avoid real trouble and try to listen to what others have to say. You can get angry quite quickly, but you do not hold grudges. However, while you are angry you can act rashly and may say things that you will regret later. In talking with other people, you prefer to be simple and direct - just be careful not to be so blunt that you hurt people's feelings.

You would benefit by learning to slow down, relax, and just let things be sometimes, but your energetic, restless nature rarely allows you to do this. You need to learn to control your impulsiveness and restlessness. You must try not to become so easily irritated and angered, and to seek positive and creative outlets for your natural aggressiveness. Because your mind is so active and you are always thinking of the next thing, you sometimes appear to have an intolerant and snappy

9

attitude, which you are not always aware of. Try and learn to think about others, considering their ideas and needs without losing your own values and love of yourself. The four lessons you should learn are: patience, conservation of energy, finishing what you start, and control of your temper. The natural tendency for an Arian is to stand alone and do everything themselves; however, being receptive and appreciative of others' contributions, ideas, and feelings would go a long way in enhancing your relationships.

Taurus

The Bull
21st April – 21st May

Taurus is the Fixed Earth sign. Fixed signs are resistant to change and Earth signs are practical. You are therefore very patient and like to do things slowly so that you can see what is really happening. You probably find it difficult to change course once you have started something, and you can be very obstinate. You don't mind working a long time for the results you want, but you need to understand and relate to those results. You also need to see the point of things that you do; you find it difficult to work on vague objectives that don't seem to benefit you.

You like to be comfortable, and with your love of comfort and ease you may try to avoid strenuous situations, but you really need such experiences to help you mature. You can be slow to change your opinions, but once they have changed it is very difficult to change them back. You need time to assimilate experiences and mull things over.

You have a natural love of all living things, and you like getting your hands on your work, building things, and seeing the tangible, practical results of your effort. You may have an artistic or musical aptitude. Because you like to do everything thoroughly, you sometimes appear to work at a slower pace than some other people, but you always finish whatever projects you start. You are likely to work well with your hands because you take the trouble to do everything correctly. Because of this, you are reliable, trustworthy, careful and steadfast. You are better at sustaining what others have started rather than starting things yourself. You can be led, but never pushed. You are never in a hurry. You hate being forced or rushed into a decision or an action, especially if you have not been given time to think it all through and evaluate the practicalities of the situation. You generally succeed at what you do, because you have the ability to concentrate and follow a project through to its completion. Mentally, you are keen-witted and practical more than intellectual, but you can become fixed in your opinions through your preference for following accepted and reliable patterns of experience. Your character is generally dependable, steadfast, prudent, just, firm and unshaken in the face of difficulties. In times of crisis, you are generally cool and collected and have the patience and ability to come up with practical solutions to problems.

You love beautiful things, and you probably find that possessions and material things are of great significance to you. This is possibly because you don't feel emotionally secure unless you can see and touch the objects you own. People will like you because you are affectionate; you give and receive love easily. However, if others try to take advantage of your serenity, they will quickly discover that, when you are roused to anger, you don't calm down easily. You get a sense of security from your stable life values and your physical possessions. Owning property also makes you feel secure and you probably worry about falling into debt; therefore, you will do everything in your power to maintain the security of the status quo and you won't want things in your life to change.

You can sometimes have fixed ideas and be very tenacious, especially if things don't go as planned. You sometimes find it difficult to accept opinions that are different to your own, so you need to learn to be more flexible and open-minded. Be aware that you can go to extremes on occasion, such as sometimes being too attached to the principles you admire. If you are provoked, you can explode into outbursts of anger, but these generally don't last long. One of your lessons is to be aware that you have the desire to possess people emotionally and physically. You need to learn to let this go and try and focus on mental and spiritual things. You will eventually learn detachment and then be willing to let go of people and things. Have an aim to be more flexible and try and adapt to changes in your life without feeling you must always keep control of everything.

Gemini

The Twins
22nd May – 21st June

Gemini is the Mutable Air sign. Mutable signs are adaptable and Air signs are linked to communication and understanding. You therefore always need plenty of intellectual stimulation and will probably have a continual stream of books and ideas running through your life. You will have a duality to your nature and will almost continually have to decide between two or more courses of action. Your active mind constantly moves from one subject to another and you will always remain youthful, both physically and mentally.

You are quick to observe and learn, full of restless curiosity and always seek fresh experiences. Your tendency to skim the surface should be watched, however; you should try to finish anything you start. You enjoy, and need, work that includes a great deal of variety. You love being involved in several things at once but having too many irons in the fire at the same time may cause you problems - it often makes you late for appointments, for example! You are always on the go, and you can very easily become bored; your answer to this tends to be to drop whatever is boring you and move on to the next job in hand. You will therefore tend to flit from one experience to another, gathering all types of information along the way, but seldom getting to the real details of any subject. You need to learn to concentrate your energy or you could be a 'jack of all trades' and not completely master anything. However, it is no good trying to tie you down to routine work, for this will only lead to nervous exhaustion. You need to do something in which there is plenty of change, movement and travel.

Your thought processes are quick, and you have the ability to use the right words in any situation. You possess great wit and a good sense of humour. Other people may have difficulty in keeping up with your rapid change of subjects. Because you think so quickly, you often finish other people's sentences for them, but this can be most frustrating for the person trying to express their own thoughts! You need to learn how to control the urge to jump in and allow slower people to express their own opinions and ideas.

Since you have the ability to see both sides of any issue, you may fluctuate back and forth between opposing viewpoints. You will probably tend to side with the opinion of whomever you happen to be with at that particular moment, then you change as the circumstances change - indecisiveness can be a problem for you. You have so much nervous energy that this can sometimes cause great stress which must find an appropriate release.

You need to be aware that you can tend to lose energy through lack of concentration and having too many projects on the go. You need a quiet, regular routine, though this is hard for you as you tend to live on your nerves and love plenty of mental stimulation. A lesson for you is to learn self-discipline so as not to overstrain your sensitive and highly strung nervous system.

Cancer

The Crab
22nd June – 22nd July

Cancer is the Cardinal Water sign. Cardinal signs like to start things and Water signs are emotional and intuitive. Therefore, your heart must be in a project fully before you can be interested enough to start it and totally commit to the work involved. You like to plan for the future, and you need security. You probably have an excellent memory. You are sometimes shy and can occasionally find it hard to make friends, but once your affection has been won you are constant and devoted. You have a natural tendency to be self-sufficient and don't mind being alone, so you must make an effort to socialise. You tend to cling to familiar places and people, and you can be apprehensive at the thought of any changes and upheaval in your domestic life. You also love the past and, at times, find a lot of fulfilment in it. This is why, when you have new experiences, you always want to return to something familiar. This can be a problem sometimes, though, as you also may find that your preoccupation with the past can cause you to hold on to the memories of things that went wrong in your life. You are sensitive, though you may not always show this. Arguments tend to wear you down, criticisms can hurt you and you can find yourself hiding away from things that create conflict in your life.

You often need to get a lot of protection and comfort from your environment. You tend to cling to that which provides security: the past, possessions, your home and family. Cut off from your safe background, you can feel exposed and vulnerable, and you then tend to keep other people at bay. Because you are very sensitive and easily hurt, you can find yourself caught in emotional scenes and irrational behaviour. You could have the habit of looking ahead and behind you at the same time, not fully wanting to face the future head-on and often worrying about the past and what might be sneaking up on you from behind, which causes you anxiety.

You tend to generally respond to life through your emotions rather than through your mind. You can sometimes let your emotions rule you, and thus operate from an emotional point of view instead of a more rational one. You will absorb the emotional vibrations of wherever you are, so it is important to be in positive environments as much as possible. Because you often live in your feelings, you have a strong need to feel secure; home and family bring the highest sense of security for you. Because of this, it is necessary for you to know that the people you love also care about you. You are probably well-known in your social group for being changeable – you can change your mind, your mood, or anything really! However, you will achieve a lot if you can think positively and try not to dwell in the past. You have strong determination and great perseverance, and if you use these qualities for constant effort then you can attain your goals and free yourself of worry.

You do need to be aware that you often keep your worries to yourself, rejecting the release of talking them over with others, and the resulting tension often upsets your sensitive digestive system. A lesson for you is to learn to find ways to release some of your stress and be more aware of your emotions and how they influence your temperament. Another challenge is for you to develop independence and wise judgment, so that your natural shrewdness can guide you to the right path.

Leo

The Lion
23rd July – 22nd August

Leo is the Fixed Fire sign. Fixed signs are resistant to change and Fire signs are enthusiastic and passionate. You are therefore optimistic and cheerful (you really do bring sunshine into other people's lives), but you can have a closed mind to new ideas. You also have a pronounced sense of drama and usually like to be the centre of attention. You are a hard worker and can set a good example to others. You are often sensitive and easily hurt, although you would never show it. You can have a tendency to want what everyone else has. You often have a need to recharge your abundant energy, and at these times you may appear quiet and withdrawn.

You are good-hearted and immensely generous. Your intentions are always good, and you're honest, sincere and genuinely kind. Other people are generally fond of you, even though you can sometimes use them to show off your own success. You can be a master at delegating disagreeable duties in order to concentrate on the more important, creative (i.e. more amusing) tasks, but then you probably do them better than anyone else! You can be a warm, convincing, entertaining speaker and an effective storyteller. You don't do very well alone; you need to motivate and interact with others. Although you seem strong on the outside, you are actually sensitive and your feelings are easily hurt. Generally, you have good health with strong recuperative powers. You are seldom sad, but, when you are, you find it overwhelming. Fortunately, you are very resilient so are soon sunny and happy again.

You probably choose to do things that give you a wide scope for creativity, organising, and leadership, but you do need structure so that you don't waste your energy in counter-productive activities. You will have a decided flair for the dramatic, being the centre of attention, having a good time, and running everything. You are never mean or spiteful, but you know how to get your own way if you need to. No matter what your actions, you always have the belief that whatever you do is for the other person's benefit. However, you are very honest and reluctant to compromise yourself. You thrive on challenge but to others your behaviour can sometimes appear to be meddling or small-minded.

You are not timid, meek, or self-effacing, and you are rarely content being in the background or in the subordinate position. You are a natural leader and do not take orders from others very well. You must have something of your own, something creative – be it a business, a project, a home or whatever – that you can develop and manage according to your own will and vision. Whatever you do, you do it in a unique, dramatic, individual way; you like to put your own personal stamp on it.

You are courageous, affectionate and powerful, but you should get into the habit of reassessing your opinion as often as possible, and ensure you are making good use of your natural, spontaneous charm. You must try not to be intolerant and fixed in your opinions. Important lessons for you are to understand and recognise your limitations and for you to understand self-discipline so you can think before you act.

Virgo

The Virgin
23rd August – 22nd September

Virgo is the Mutable Earth sign. Mutable signs are adaptable and Earth signs are practical. Therefore, you are a hard worker, with a great deal of common sense, and you are practical with a flair for meticulous work. You like to work with a lot of details, usually of a technical or analytical nature, in and for the service of others. You do not have to be the boss as service is more important to you than leadership. Also, you are likely to be good with your hands, because you work very carefully to reach a high standard of craftsmanship. If you cannot do something well, you are not likely to do it at all. You tend to strive for perfection, and often feel a vague sense of dissatisfaction and a lack of confidence when you feel you haven't achieved this. You are indecisive, or, having made a decision, you always look back and worry if you've done the right thing. You do tend to be fussy and to worry, and you should try and avoid being too critical of others as this is something you can do without thinking sometimes. However, you do like to be noticed by others and to have your efforts acknowledged.

What you do is important to you and you work conscientiously, methodically and thoroughly, not letting your dedicated application to detail cloud more important issues. You're clever and a quick learner, intellectual and practical, tidy and analytical. You are very careful in everything you do, and you put a high value on neatness; because of this, you often expect others to live up to those same high standards, and you can get disappointed if they do not. When you see something wrong in someone or something, you sometimes have a tendency to point it out, but you usually manage to be considerate when you do this because you know that criticising others can upset them.

You are very interested in learning as much as possible about the world. In whatever you make or do, you apply the same standards of excellence that you want other people to live up to. You like to help others because being useful makes you feel good. You are able to put off what you want for yourself in order to help someone you love do what he or she wants, and others will respect you for this. You have a curious and inquiring mind with an excellent memory, and you instinctively scrutinise everything. You enjoy analysing people, situations, and problems. You always want to know how, why, when and where. You have a flair for organisation and enjoy setting up schedules.

You tend to search constantly for worthy goals to pursue and may pose large questions, but you are sometimes reluctant to take large risks. Cautious and conservative, you generally prefer small-scale plans to grand strategies. You are rooted in the present and amenable to change only after thinking things through carefully, but this is generally because you don't want to be disappointed.

You would benefit by learning to let up on your constant activity – usually, your idea of relaxation seems like hard work to everyone else! In your quest for perfection in details, you can all too easily lose sight of the overall picture and this can cause you unnecessary stress and wasted energy. You need to learn to examine every experience and integrate it without regret or resentment. Sometimes you may feel that your life is missing something, and this can make you feel 'not good enough' or a bit sad. Let these feelings go, if you can. You are not inadequate and it is only your drive for perfection that makes you feel that way.

Libra

The Scales
23rd September – 22nd October

Libra is the Cardinal Air sign. Cardinal signs like to start things and Air signs are linked to communication and understanding. You therefore feel most fulfilled when in a partnership or in situations where you can adjust or work with human relationships, as you don't like feeling alone. Pleasant surroundings are important to you and you are a natural, cheerful optimist. You will do best in an emotional relationship in which the give-and-take is well balanced. You're sociable, charming and popular, and you don't like quarrels; you will do anything to avoid one – sometimes to the extent of compromising yourself to avoid conflict. You probably find it hard to remain emotionally stable if there is disagreement around you. This leads to you wanting peace at any price, which can sometimes encourage others to take advantage of you.

Although you like to weigh the pros and cons of a situation before you come to any conclusion, if this is taken too far you can get to the point where you can't come up with any conclusion at all, which makes you seem indecisive. Remember, if you wait too long to make a decision, you may miss many excellent opportunities. You can also appear indecisive because you see clearly all sides of every problem, so you find it extremely difficult to decide which side to take. Your instinct is usually right and could help you to reach a decision. A lesson for you is to try to form your own opinions, because you can be easily swayed by the views of others, and sometimes you could even come to rely on a stronger character to form your opinions for you.

You want to be liked by everyone, as you are so sociable, and if you are asked for help you can give sound, practical advice as you are able to see the entire problem. But, because you want to get along with everyone, you may have difficulty saying "no" sometimes. You may then find that a stronger personality could potentially overshadow you; therefore you should develop your self-reliance and stand up for your own beliefs and principles. However, you have a natural ability to keep the peace and win people over. You do have an instinctive sense of fairness, though, and can be diplomatic, balanced and cooperative - a natural mediator.

You hate to see imbalance and injustice in the world or to see problems with anything, and you will naturally try and restore harmony, order and balance. But sometimes it is necessary to fight, and you should learn when and how to do so.

You probably find that aesthetic appearances

matter a lot to you, and you love to be in beautiful places, surrounded by magnificent things. You really do care about the way things look; you don't like harsh or dirty conditions and you tend to put off a decision (or mildly unsavoury job) for as long as possible. But you always show polite, civilised behaviour and want to do the right thing as much as possible. Just be careful not to take appeasement too far.

Scorpio

The Scorpion
23rd October – 21st November

Scorpio is the Fixed Water sign. Fixed signs are resistant to change and Water signs are emotional and intuitive. Therefore, you tend to be a very determined, strong-willed person who has a need to influence others. If you don't succeed in winning people over with your powerful magnetic attraction, which is quite hard to resist, you may reach for stronger weapons such as your astute mind, remarkable perception and intense energy. You have a quick mind and sharp wit, which often produces accurate sarcastic remarks. You can be a bit suspicious of some people or situations and sometimes lead your life as others play poker – few people can guess what really goes on inside you.

You are passionate in all areas of your life, and a unique intensity permeates your whole personality, giving you an extremely strong sense of purpose in life and a determination to do nothing by halves. You must live your life to the full and will probably over-indulge yourself, not only in play but in work, too. Because you feel things so strongly, you can sometimes be a bit jealous, and not only in love -whoever holds a position to which you feel entitled could be unpopular with you. Your enormously powerful energy gives you hidden depths which are often unsuspected by less emotional people. If you can learn to properly channel this force it will give you great qualities of endurance; you will battle endlessly to achieve your goals.

You also have the power to rise above worldly difficulties and to soar away from earthbound problems. This side of your personality will make you avoid dull occupations, and you will be quick to adapt to turning points in your life: when you come to such a point, you will find it easy to accept that one path has ended and will willingly turn to another. You may even force yourself to leave one road and embark on another, working hard to build a career and thus, for reasons obscure to others as they are profound to you, destroy what you have built in order to start again.

You have a strong will and a determination to

achieve anything you embark on. You have an analytical mind, strong intuition, reasoning powers, perception, long range planning ability, magnetism and energy, and also very definite opinions! These opinions can be so rigid that no amount of persuasion will make you change your mind. You are very responsive to challenge and can overcome most difficulties, although you like acknowledgement for taking the lead and rewards for your achievements.

You tend to make friends easily and be very supportive of them as you are very attached to your friends. In these relationships, you like to know what their plans are, but, because of your tendency to secretiveness, you do not necessarily want them to know what you are planning. You are capable of extreme self-sacrifice for those you love. It is usually difficult to deceive you because your intuition enables you to understand the motives of other people. You receive very strong first impressions of others, experiencing an immediate liking or a dislike for the person involved.

You need to learn flexibility, both in thought and action. Once your course of action is set, it is difficult for you to change. Trivial things bore you and you like to go deeply into things that interest you – the more intense, the better. In whatever you do, you want to be completely engrossed. Half-hearted measures are not for you. You would benefit from learning to control your powerful feelings and emotions, to subdue your stubborn and obstinate attitudes, and to develop a sense of purpose.

Sagittarius

The Archer
22nd November – 21st December

Sagittarius in the Mutable Fire sign. Mutable signs are adaptable and Fire signs are enthusiastic and passionate. Therefore, you are always full of enthusiasm. You tend to show this enthusiasm more at the start of new endeavours, then it usually lessens as the project goes along and gets stuck in details, or the going gets a little rough, or it simply gets a little boring. You take life as you find it. With high spirits and unflinching optimism, you indulge in a number of different pursuits, interests, hobbies and projects. You always assume that help will turn up when it is needed, and, for you, it usually does. You're benevolent, good-natured and humorous and will always remain youthful, both physically and mentally. You love adventure, long journeys and new, exciting experiences. Your straightforward manner can occasionally land you in trouble – you could unintentionally be blunt and tactless, and you are then surprised when people are upset by what you've said as you never mean any harm. You tend to be clumsy with material things, perhaps because they're not all that important to you. Your friendly surface goes with a philosophical outlook on life and your integrity is usually above reproach. All humanistic subjects could appeal to you and you are often interested in academic professions. Generally, you are wise and give good advice. You tend to be freedom-loving and rebellious if made to do something you don't want to do. You thrive on impossible challenges and like to win against the odds. You resent having random restrictions put on you, but if things (such as rules) are explained and you understand them, then you are usually able to follow them. You have to agree with something before you can do it.

You tend to be philosophical and you want to understand the deeper issues and concepts of life. You have a certain faith in higher things that, generally, always keeps you optimistic no matter what difficulties you are currently experiencing. You want to understand the meaning of life. This helps to keep you growing and expanding, which is something you need to do. However, this desire for expansion can cause you to overextend yourself with too many activities, and you may use up your energy too rapidly. You need to learn how to concentrate on your current projects and stick with them to the end. You also need to take intervals of rest to recuperate between projects.

Career-wise, you are reluctant to become tied

down to a set schedule, so will experiment with a variety of jobs. You generally do best in occupations that permit you to travel about, either locally or widely. You also like dealing directly with people, either selling or promoting ideas, products, etc. You may overlook small details, but your overall sense of planning is excellent and you have a good memory. The challenge of a problem is what interests you, for it caters to your enjoyment in exploring the unknown. Playing games comes easily to you and it is the journey you enjoy rather than the destination.

You will benefit from learning to discriminate between true intuition and hasty conclusions, at which you sometimes arrive impulsively when you have not bothered to think things through. You need to learn a bit of self-control in your life and work on decreasing your restlessness and tendency to exaggerate.

Capricorn

The Goat
22nd December – 20th January

Capricorn is the Cardinal Earth sign. Cardinal signs like to start things and Earth signs are practical. Therefore, your ambition can be tremendous. Early in life you decide upon a course and then hold onto it throughout your life, working methodically and conscientiously. You know what you want and how to get it. You're dutiful and tenacious so it's not surprising that, sooner or later, you achieve exactly what you had in mind. You take yourself seriously, but that side of your character may be concealed under a delightful, modest, charming image, which on occasions can develop into frivolity. You love having deep discussions about anything, as long as it doesn't touch upon your private life - that is something you would rather keep to yourself.

You like to plan your every move, weighing all the pros and cons of any issue in advance. You are dependable, particularly in a crisis. When asked, you give sound, practical advice. You are, as a rule, not aggressive, and only express hostility as a defence when attacked.

At times, you can be very sensitive and can feel alone, as if no one understands you; however, you do need people, but you tend to isolate yourself from others due to your reserve and fear of being hurt. You can be very loyal to close friends and people you care about. Respect and recognition are important to you and encouragement and praise are essential for motivating you.

You have strong self-discipline, and nothing turns you from your course if your mind is made up. You will even give up many pleasures in order to reach your goals; hard work invigorates you. You are thrifty and like to collect things, and you hate waste; this includes wasting a lot of talk in idle chatter – you only speak when you have something to say! Because you are self-contained, you may feel alone even when in relationships, as you can find emotions difficult. This may be due to a fault in communication due to shyness, or because you consider work to be more important. But, whatever the reason, you will tend to feel alone unless you make a real effort to be less serious in your partnerships.

You can be very creative, but you must learn to overcome your own self-doubts and lack of confidence - not trusting your own abilities can hold you back. You must learn to believe in yourself and become more optimistic. There is no mountain you cannot climb if that is what you desire to do. Once your mind is made up you can achieve great things and you get a feeling of security from your achievements.

You tend to have a lot of patience - which is good, because sometimes your plans meet with delays, setbacks and obstacles. This teaches you tolerance, which therefore encourages you to strive for spiritual fulfilment rather than material fulfilment. For you, work is therapeutic and is probably the best medicine for whatever ails you, but you are prone to overworking, which you must try not to do. However, it is difficult for you to really relax; you are happiest when busy, even in your spare time.

You will benefit from trying to be more flexible and having a bit more fun in your life. A lesson for you is not to over-estimate your capabilities, as you can sometimes try to do too much. You can feel very driven a lot of the time, but letting go of this sometimes will also benefit you.

Aquarius

The Water Bearer
21st January – 19th February

Aquarius is the Fixed Air sign. Fixed signs are resistant to change and Air signs are linked to communication and understanding. Therefore, you will always have an original streak, and be in favour of reform which often shows as an interest in 'causes'. However, you can be stubborn: modern in outlook but fixed in opinion. You have an independent charm that others find fascinating and dynamic, but you can sometimes appear to be indifferent and distant, even though you generally have a joyful nature. You are kind and friendly, but can be rather aloof and frequently unpredictable. A feeling of space is important to you; you are ready to help others at a moment's notice, but you will always remain personally detached, and sometimes it can be difficult for others to feel close to you because of this. Personal independence is of enormous importance to you and you are capable of making great sacrifices for it, even to the point of rejecting relationships. More conventional people may find themselves at odds with you because of this, and because of your unpredictability. You can sometimes feel frustrated if you think that other people don't understand you.

You usually have clear-cut objectives in life and generally achieve them successfully. A lot of your time is likely to be spent in societies and group activities. Your friendships will usually be rewarding and you are likely to bring happiness to others.

You are warm-hearted and generous, with a charming disposition. You may be inclined towards the arts, particularly music. Others feel at ease in your company. However, you're so secure and self-sufficient that you see no need to compromise just to protect a relationship, and so you could spend more time single than your friends do. Your personal goals in life can be boosted by your ability to use your charm and powers of persuasion. Your instinctive talent for gaining attention - even being a bit flamboyant when the occasion calls for it - encourages other people to give you what you want. You have strength and health. Your energy can find an intellectual outlet, and you have an ability to reach quick decisions. You are tolerant, broad-minded and have a refreshing lack of prejudice.

You seek to share knowledge with others in order to bring about a better life for all; helping others so they can help themselves appeals to you. You can get excited about bringing new ideas and methods into old, traditional environments. You are philosophical, visionary and idealistic, and feelings of friendship drive you to try to improve the life of everyone you can.

You have the determination and persistence to get ahead, but sometimes your energy level is relatively low which causes you to drop projects before they are completed. Your mind is analytical and scientific, and you have the ability to think things through to an accurate conclusion. Although you generally have good powers of concentration and are able to assimilate a lot of information, there are times when you are just plain absentminded. However, you don't like it when other people attempt to interfere in your thought processes.

You usually get along well with others; you are generally not a gossip, nor are you petty. You do not like arguments unless you feel there is a need to defend a person, an ideal or a principle. Since you are so willing to listen to the new and different, you have little patience with those who refuse to hear new concepts.

Sometimes you might rebel just for the pleasure of it and may deliberately do things in an attempt to shock people. You prefer not to be bound by schedules and regulations but can easily adapt to them if you must, though you are unlikely to be on time for things! You have an unusual way of doing things and will often refuse to do something the 'normal' way since you have a very individualistic approach to life. You also can't be forced to do something; you will need to choose to do it for yourself and work through things in your own way.

You tend to struggle with people who are possessive of you, since you are generally not possessive of people or things yourself. You give others a lot of personal freedom and you expect the same in return. Since you are not particularly concerned as to what other people think of you, you often do not bother forming opinions about other people's behaviour.

When you are with a group of friends, you think about the group as a whole rather than just about yourself. This can cause problems for you if your needs conflict with the needs of the rest of the group, but you will stand up for anyone who is not being treated fairly. You tend to look to other people for life experience, rather than books or situations, as you are convinced that everyone has something of value to teach.

You will benefit from overcoming your tendency to be unpredictable, rebellious, outspoken and fixed in your opinions. You sometimes seem mysterious and confusing and other people find it difficult to understand you, but, actually, you often don't really understand yourself. Therefore, you should work on developing your self-awareness. Due to your liking of new things and new ideas, you get bored by old ways of thinking and acting, and this needs to be controlled or you may find yourself giving up on something before you have a chance to see its benefits.

Pisces

The Fish
20th February – 20th March

Pisces is the Mutable Water sign. Mutable signs are adaptable and Water signs are emotional and intuitive. Therefore, you are very susceptible to outside influences. You are very sensitive indeed, and also innocent and impractical. You have great compassion and an ability to relieve the suffering of others. It will not be easy for you to conform; you cannot cope very well with discipline or routine and will not run your life in anything like an orderly manner. However, your natural charm, kindness, sympathy and genuine 'softness' will overcome any chaos that abounds in your life. Your sentimentality can sometimes annoy more practical, down-to-earth people, but your devotion and helpfulness to others could inspire more materialistic types.

Your basic desire is to let things happen on their own and in this way you can be effective without acting. You are a very perceptive and emotional person who quickly picks up moods and emotions from other people and makes them part of your own. This trait makes it very easy for others to hurt your feelings. Because you have the ability to put yourself in someone else's place, you have an exceptional understanding of other people's needs. Whenever possible, you try to help others, because it makes you feel good about yourself.

Very often you like to go into your own private fantasy world and think about ideas that mean something only to you. Just be careful that you don't spend so much time there so as not to lose track of what is happening outside in the real world. You may be somewhat shy because you feel you have to trust people before you can really open up to them. But even though you are a bit shy, you do need other people, for without them you feel lonely, even in your own private world.

Your impulse is to go with the flow. You tend to absorb the information and environment around you and can adjust to new situations easily. Therefore, it is important that you surround yourself with uplifting people and circumstances. You are creative and self-sufficient, and your mind is extremely active due to your strong imagination, although you can sometimes get carried away. You sense and feel things that others are not aware of. Your nerves and mental health require you to periodically rest away from the noise of the everyday world. You need sufficient time each day to be alone while you recharge your fluctuating energies, so take some time to be alone with yourself to regroup - not too much time, as you can sometimes get carried away with yourself and your problems.

Your instinctive desire to 'escape' can be used constructively through creativity. You have a very rich imagination, and you love to spend time daydreaming and making up fantasies. You can put your imagination to good use in writing stories or poems, as you can see the world in ways that are hidden from many others. You may lack a strong desire to work or to push yourself into doing anything that takes a lot of strength, organisation, patience, and responsibility. You dislike being pinned down to facts and you follow your instinct rather than logic.

You would benefit from being particularly discriminating and careful in your choice of companions, as you find it so difficult not to absorb other people's characteristics. Since you tend to be easily confused and unable to manage practicalities, you need to learn coping and everyday skills, as well as learning to overcome your inclinations to be vague, careless and secretive. There is a tendency for you to gravitate toward becoming a 'jack-of-all-trades'; concentrating on one specific aim will aid you in gaining success. However, your heart must be in a project fully before you can be interested enough to totally commit to the work involved. Thus, you should always be free to choose things that you really love. A lesson for you is to learn to have fun and be more playful; re-capture your childhood.

HOW TO APPROACH BEING MINDFUL

Wherever you are, be there totally ~ Eckhart Tolle

There are many different books around now that talk about mindfulness and how to do it (you're reading one!) However, these never seem to give many options for people. It can sometimes appear to be a very structured process with specific guidelines, and people who are new to the whole process can find it daunting. The most important thing is not to get too bogged down by details. It doesn't matter what you do, or how you do it, or how long you do it for - what matters the most is the intent.

There are many different techniques that help us to be mindful, which we'll cover later. To start with, though, we need to consider our thoughts. We need to be able to let go of any negative or unhelpful thoughts when we are practising mindfulness. We have a constant, endless stream of thoughts that run through our head all of the time and we need to find a way to stop these thoughts from gaining prominence in our mind. These thoughts come from our Ego. Our 'real' selves live in our subconscious most of the time, and the conscious mind is run by our Ego. It is really important to remember that we are not our Ego. Mindfulness is a way of removing the Ego, or at least getting it out of the way for a while. We all identify with our Ego, and while we live our everyday lives - caught up in meeting deadlines, wanting new stuff and letting our emotions go unchecked - we are not living with awareness, discipline or attention. We need to be able to step outside of the boundaries of the Ego (picture the Ego in a box in your conscious mind) so that we can take an objective look at ourselves and our lives. The Ego does not want to be bypassed in this way, and we will find it will keep putting up reasons not to be mindful. Studies show that we are usually not aware of how often our Ego can mislead us. If we just accept everything our Ego says, we won't be able to tell what is true and what is not; we will think that everything our Ego says is real. Some people are genuinely convinced that they already have an accurate picture of reality and that they see things exactly as they are. Such people obviously haven't had enough experiences to realise that their mind can be deceptive. For example, although we literally can't see what's in our blind spot (the area in our visual field where some nerves connect to the retina), our brain fills in this gap with an 'educated guess' so we are not truly 'seeing' what is there, but we wouldn't know this from our experience. Also, as lots of research shows, we are programmed to see patterns, even if they don't actually exist, leading us to infer meaning into totally random events. What these studies reveal is that, in assuming whatever we believe is the truth and the only truth, we are unaware of a major source of delusion: our mind. This is not to say that the mind always deludes us. Rather, if we unquestioningly accept everything that our mind says, we won't be able to tell when our mind is deluding us from when it is not.

Some people also raise other objections or obstacles to the idea of practising mindfulness. One objection that some people have to mindfulness is they think it is a Buddhist practice or a Hindu practice. But, really, everyone has thoughts and feelings, and if we deny ourselves the opportunity to engage in mindfulness because we feel it is not part of our religion, then I think we are denying ourselves a very powerful source of well-being. Another obstacle can be that we think that mindfulness will make us 'soft' or 'weak'. It's true that it will make us kinder and more compassionate, but hopefully we don't equate kind and compassionate with weakness (which unfortunately some people still do). Also, these same people think that those who turn to mindfulness can't cope with the stresses of daily life, so they conclude that it is mindfulness itself that must make people weak. If we find our Ego trying to get us to take any of these objections seriously, we must just ignore it! And if we find we are having doubts about the wisdom of trying to be mindful we should keep remembering that it is our Ego bringing up objections.

When many of us think of mindfulness, one of our first thoughts is that we have to stop thinking. Mindfulness is not about 'not thinking'; rather, it's about changing our relationship with our thoughts. Specifically, the goal is trying not to get caught up in our thoughts, which is what happens when we judge, categorise, or comment on a thought. So, the aim is to separate ourselves from our thoughts and feelings, and other aspects of our Ego, and to merely observe them as if we were observing clouds passing by in the sky, or as if we were guards at Buckingham Palace, merely observing the tourists without passing judgment on them or getting entangled in a conversation with them. Some researchers refer to this idea of 'merely observing' as 'bare awareness'. Bare awareness means we're trying to be aware without getting caught up in our thoughts, feelings, etc. However, unless we actually start mindfulness practice, we won't realise what it means to merely observe our thoughts and feelings. Because mindfulness is such a difficult concept to understand intellectually, and because many people want to know what they're getting into before they're willing to do it, many of us are reluctant to try out mindfulness. This can then lead to a catch-22 situation, because we won't try mindfulness until we get to experience what it can lead to first, but without trying it out first we may never get to experience what it is all about.

Another obstacle is time. A lot of people worry that it will take weeks, months, or even years before we get to see what mindfulness can do for us, and this also prevents them from trying it. However, a large research project proved that just being mindful for five minutes a day for five weeks can be enough to cause the changes in our brain that develop when positive emotions increase. Therefore, this is the goal that I want us to aim for.

We can sometimes discover barriers when we try to find the time, space and energy to make mindfulness a regular practice. Most of us lead such hectic lives that we don't find enough time to do anything that we consider relaxing, such as taking a proper lunch break or playing with the children. So, fitting in a mindfulness session every day may be asking for too much. However, remember that initially our goal is to only do five minutes of mindfulness a day. Ideally, this would be all in one go, but it doesn't have to be - at least not at the beginning. We are much better off doing a very short session (one or two minutes) so that we can actually achieve what we set out to do. This is more successful than aiming for half an hour and fidgeting for most of that time or worrying about what we are not getting done. Then, as we get familiar with the techniques and become more used to the practices we can gradually increase the time.

Sometimes you can get frustrated with mindfulness, especially if we go into it with high expectations – we've read all about the benefits and we want to experience them for ourselves. We will then start to compare what we are actually experiencing with what we think we should be experiencing. In some situations - for example achieving high marks in a test - comparing where we are with where we want to be can be a good thing. But, in other situations, it is not a good thing to make this comparison as it can hurt our chances of achieving our goal. Mindfulness is like this. The more we constantly monitor and compare where we are with where we want to be, the less likely we will get there.

The good news about knowing the benefits of mindfulness is that this can motivate us to get started; the bad news is knowing these benefits can set high expectations which may get in the way of being mindful – in turn, this can lead to frustration. So we should just do what we can, try not to have any expectations, and see what happens.

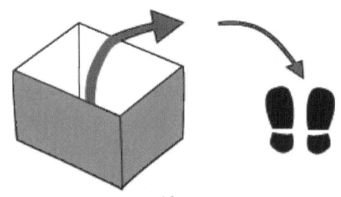

Step outside your ego

THE BENEFITS OF MINDFULNESS

You can't stop the waves, but you can learn to surf
~ Jon Kabat-Zinn

So you now have an awareness of what mindfulness is and how to achieve it, but before you start any of the practices it might be useful to identify why you want to be mindful. Research suggests that, in general, most people take up mindfulness because they think it will help them increase their sense of well-being and manage their emotions better. Others try it because they think they will be calmer and feel happier, more fulfilled and self-aware; a few people try it because other people have told them they might like it, and a small minority take it up because they associate it with religious or spiritual development - particularly Buddhism. Once you identify the reason behind your initial interest, you can use that to keep your motivation and keep reminding yourself of your goal.

Research shows that practising mindfulness

will make you happier; therefore, being mindful makes us happy. Or, to put it differently, we're happy when we are in a state of mindfulness. Basically, positive and negative emotions manifest differently in the brain - when we're feeling happy we have higher left to right energy ratios in our prefrontal cortex, and when we're feeling unhappy or anxious we see much greater activity in the right to left energy ratio in the prefrontal cortex. This was subsequently researched on many people, one of whom was a Tibetan monk, and they found that his left to right energy ratio was much higher than any of the other people they had studied. The question was then raised: was the monk born happy, or did the many hours he spent meditating have an effect on his happiness? So, they did another research study with people who had never meditated before and put them into two groups: one group who did regular mindfulness practice, and a control group who did nothing differently. Then, after four months, the researchers studied the brains of the two groups and found that there were significant differences in the left to right energy ratio of the people in the mindfulness group. This proves that our repeated experiences shape our brain. When we practise mindfulness, the parts of the brain that are involved with attention, concentration, emotional intelligence and compassion get stronger and bigger - this is called cortical thickening. Cortical thickening is linked to practice – what we practise gets stronger. Imagine we have a 'thought and emotion' motorway in our brain, and this is the road we automatically use, out of habit. When we start to learn something new, we need to make a new road –we will probably begin by clearing away the overgrown vegetation, and then walking on the grass to create a path, and then putting gravel on the path we have made etc. Each time we do the new thing, our new road gets a bit more established, until eventually it rivals the motorway and the new road becomes the habit. As well as this, a great side benefit of cortical thickening is that our brain ages less rapidly than it otherwise would.

Practising mindfulness (and being happier) will reduce stress and anxiety and increase our physical health. Physical health improves in many ways: our immune system becomes stronger, skin conditions (like psoriasis) improve, and things like blood pressure, arrhythmia (irregular heartbeat) and other symptoms of poor heart health are all improved. We will be less tired, we will sleep better and we will have more resistance to pain. Another major physiological benefit of mindfulness is that it has been shown to prevent the shortening of something called telomeres in the cells of our bodies. Telomeres protect the ends of chromosomes, and thus help prevent the onset of diseases like cancer.

Mindfulness also helps us to improve mentally – we will have quicker mental processing skills, enhanced concentration, memory improvement and increased intuition. We become more self-aware, more confident, more decisive, more grounded; we can release negative thoughts about ourselves and stop acting on autopilot. Mindfulness is a way of stopping our mind from wandering. It anchors us in the present moment, allowing us to acknowledge our emotions and feelings, but not to react to them or judge them. In effect we become a 'disinterested observer', as we will discuss later.

Another way in which mindfulness improves our life is by enhancing our creativity. A lot of studies have shown that we produce our best ideas when our mind is relatively calm, which is when we appear to have maximum access to all of our experiences and knowledge. When we relax we are more able to tap into all parts of our brain and make connections between two apparently unrelated thoughts or memories, which, of course, is critical for creativity. In contrast, when we feel stressed, we aren't able to make these connections as easily.

Mindfulness also promotes compassion in that it improves our ability to empathise with others by activating a part of our brain called the insular cortex. As a result, those that practice mindfulness are more selfless and altruistic. In addition to improving both physical and mental health, mindfulness not only makes us feel calmer, but also gives us an ability to react to situations in a more flexible and conscious manner, which means that we are going to respond to events in our life with a lot more emotional intelligence. And, apart from calming us down and improving our emotional intelligence by enhancing response flexibility, mindfulness also helps us to settle down into the present, which increases our ability to view even ordinary things with much more curiosity and interest. Therefore, it gives us just a little more space and time to choose how we want to react to a situation.

WHY IS MINDFULNESS SO EFFECTIVE?

The future depends on what we do in the present
~ Mahatma Ghandi

Why should mindfulness have all these positive effects? After all, trying to be mindful is to be aware of what is going on but just merely observe it. Why should being fully aware of what's going on, without judging or trying to change things, lead to all these amazing, positive effects? Mindfulness could very well have caused anxiety or led to all kinds of negative effects instead! One answer to this question - and this is the answer with which not only spiritualists but even some scientists appear to agree - is that our basic nature is one of happiness. Many religious traditions echo this idea. For example, there is a phrase in the Bible that says, "the Kingdom of God is within you". One way to interpret this phase is that we don't need to search elsewhere for salvation or happiness or bliss; it's within us. In Hinduism and Buddhism, there are even more direct references to this idea that our true nature is one of happiness or bliss.

It has been proven by research that it is good to adopt what might be considered a spiritual attitude. This includes traditional religions but also people who believe in the 'one source' or an overall 'universal energy', for example. These people have the attitude that whatever happens is for the best or it was meant to be. This attitude involves having an implicit trust in life, that we're taken care of, so that, even if we're currently experiencing a seemingly negative outcome, we'll eventually overcome it and learn, and as a result lead a happier, more meaningful and more fulfilling life. Of course, it may difficult to adopt this attitude for all events, and I certainly don't mean to say that everyone should always adopt it. But I'm sure that we can instinctively see how such an implicit faith or trust in life is going to be very helpful in moderating our reaction to difficult situations or experiences. When outcomes that appear negative happen, we'll spend far less time thinking about them or wallowing in self-pity; we'll quickly bounce back again. When we are mindful, we will develop an implicit trust in life – the belief that good things are going to happen to us and that life, by its very nature, is more benevolent rather than difficult or indifferent. What's the most rational belief to have about whether life can be trusted or not? Is it that life is good? Or is it that life is difficult? Or perhaps it is that life is indifferent? The answer turns out to be all of them! To a person who believes that 'life is good' and that 'life can be trusted,' life does turn out to be benign and trustworthy. To a person who believes the opposite, then life's experiences offer ample evidence in support of the view that life is difficult. So, therefore, from the perspective of increasing our happiness, it is better to believe that life is good, and this is where mindfulness can have the greatest impact.

There are a lot of research findings that show that those who hold a positive 'life is benign' kind of attitude, or those with a spiritual attitude towards life, are far happier than those who don't have this attitude. Likewise, findings also show that those who consider themselves lucky generally experience more positive outcomes than those who think that they're unlucky.

Remember that if we find ourselves in a behaviour pattern where we're not experiencing much joy and fulfilment in life (or not as much as we think we should), then there's no reason to believe that persisting in these same behaviours will make us any happier in the future. We must investigate how we can change if we want there to be any changes in our feelings and emotions. This means that we will have to do something new, and recognising that, until the new thing becomes familiar, it will feel uncomfortable. It's tempting to half-heartedly try a new behaviour pattern for too short a period of time and then say that it didn't work. There has been research that shows the first time we encounter anything, we don't like it very much, but the more we do it or try it, over time, the familiarity actually makes us like it more. So, we have to give new things a chance if we want the opportunity for them to make us happier. This is especially relevant to mindfulness. It is going to be very hard initially for us to find the time to be mindful or to get into the habit of practising mindfulness regularly, but if we can make these simple life changes, we will get so many benefits.

THE THREE PATHS TO MINDFULNESS

Our life is shaped by our mind, for we become what we think ~ Buddha

1. Getting in the zone, or experiencing flow

The first way that we can discover mindfulness is getting in the zone, which is also called 'experiencing flow'. 'Flow' occurs when we are doing things that have meaning to us, or that we can get engrossed in - these experiences are called flow experiences. 'Flow' means that you feel a quiet sense of control, or strength or confidence. You know what you want to achieve and how you're going to achieve it, and at the same time you don't feel worried or disturbed when you're confronted with obstacles. Many of us experience this when we engage in our hobbies, and some lucky people experience it at work too.

The first aspect of flow is a distorted perception of time. Often when we are experiencing flow, time seems to slow down, and yet when the flow experience is over it seems that time has passed really fast. When we are doing something we love, we are not aware of time at all. It is only when the flow activity has ended, or an external trigger, like our phone ringing, interrupts us that we step back and realise that we lost track of time.

The second aspect of flow is a lack of self-consciousness. When we are experiencing flow, we will be so absorbed in the activity that we will not have any thoughts left over to evaluate or judge how we are doing. We won't be comparing ourselves to others or worrying if anyone has noticed that we haven't done our hair!

The third aspect of flow is an intense focus on the present moment. Imagine that we are climbing a mountain and our plan is to climb to the summit and have a picnic lunch with a friend who is driving up there. If we were 'in flow', we wouldn't be focusing on that end goal. Our attention would be totally committed to the next step we're about to take; we would focus on the next crevice or ledge to grab hold of, or on the fact that our fingers are damp, or that there are prickly shrubs in the way. Our focus wouldn't be on what we plan to do once we reach the summit. So, in flow, our attention is focused almost entirely on the present moment.

To summarise, flow moments are characterised

by three important features: distorted perception of time, a lack of self-consciousness, and an intense focus on the present moment.

Everybody has had flow experiences, and there is actually a way we can get into flow almost whenever we want to. Flow happens in the spot between anxiety and boredom. It happens when we are challenged - not by too much, but by just the right amount. We need to stretch beyond our point of comfort, but not by too much. If we stretch too much it would be uncomfortable, and we would become anxious; if we don't stretch enough, we will not grow, and we will be bored. What this means is that as long as we're able to put ourselves in a situation where our current skill levels match the skill levels required of us (which are called the challenges), or we are stretched a little bit by the skill levels required, we will experience flow.

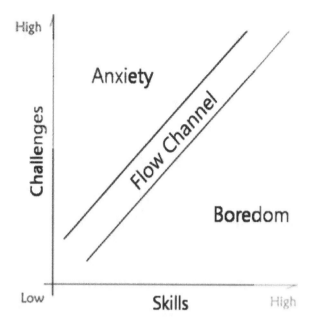

For example, we can experience flow in chess by playing against somebody who is just a little bit better than us. Or, we can experience flow in crosswords or Sudoku, or by playing the violin, and so on. We should find something that's just beyond our current capabilities, something that we find a bit difficult. However, not all situations will provide flow. It is important that we match our current skill levels with the challenge required. Imagine that we are a beginner at tennis, playing against another beginner. Given our low skill levels (and the high challenge required), we - and our tennis partner - will probably hit the ball out of the court far too often for flow to last (and we will feel anxious as a result). So, whatever flow we do experience will be disrupted by long intervals of non-flow (by retrieving the ball, mostly!) This will lead to boredom, or a lack of interest. Compare that to a situation in which both we and our opponent are expert players. At this high skill level, we are likely to sustain flow for much longer durations. Our rallies, for example, are likely to last several seconds, and in the course of these rallies we're likely to feel quite stretched. People who get to experience these high levels of flow are really lucky; they no longer have doubts about what their purpose in life is as they know it is to nurture the talent that enables them to experience this flow.

Of course, we don't always know what sort of experiences will bring us flow. Most of us lose the dreams we had as children and end up taking a practical job that will pay the bills and put food on the table, and an unfortunate consequence of this is that life loses its thrill and excitement. The truth is we can't be fully happy unless we experience flow on a regular basis. And we can't experience flow on a regular basis unless we're doing something that we find really enjoyable and challenging, at the right level.

However, there are some things that we can do right away to get more flow into our life. The most obvious thing we can do, if we aren't already doing it, is to have a hobby, or reconnect with a hobby. This is because hobbies are a great way to experience flow. If we spend two to three hours every week engaging in one, we will almost definitely experience flow. However, whatever hobby we decide to do, remember that we need to stretch ourselves in this hobby. We should ensure that we don't just do something to while away the time, but that we're actually challenged by it, and that we also really enjoy doing it. Sir Ken Robinson calls the intersection of what we enjoy doing, and what we are good at, our 'element'. As he says, one of the best ways to find fulfilment and meaning is by being in our element - doing things that we are not just good at, but that we also enjoy doing.

From a mindfulness point of view, getting into flow increases the time we spend being intensely focused on the present moment, which therefore increases mindfulness. Although we won't be doing specific 'mindfulness practice', doing something that gives us flow is a great way to start experiencing mindfulness and beginning to reap the benefits of it.

Most of us have at least one hobby or activity that we love, and, if you are Aries or Gemini, you probably have (or have had!) lots. If you already know what you enjoy doing, and it is challenging enough so that you experience flow, then that's great. Otherwise, read the notes below and have a go at as many activities as you can. There may be something that you haven't thought of trying before, which will end up being the very thing that gives you flow.

Physical Activities

Physical activities – things like sports, walking, jogging, dancing, yoga – are a great way to experience flow. Even if we find the idea of exercising daunting, there will be something physical that we can find pleasurable. For example, it may be taking a slow walk around the block with the dog, or a friend, or maybe playing a game of table tennis. It doesn't really matter what it is, as long as it gets us moving. Even if we only exercise for five minutes initially, eventually it will spur us on to continue and this will build up to longer sessions.

Astrology Signs and Physical Activities

There are many different ways we can approach doing a physical activity, so let's run through the main requirements of each sign. This will guide us in how to tailor our approach to physical activity and help us narrow down the types of activities that will suit us best. As I mentioned before, read all of the signs, as you may be more influenced by another area of your chart, not just the Sun sign. Do remember, though, that if you do not identify with the characteristics of your Sun sign, it may be that you need to build on those qualities and begin to incorporate them into your life, so don't dismiss everything out of hand just because it doesn't appeal to you at this moment in time.

• Aries

If you are Aries, you just like to get on with things and probably hate a lot of fuss or detail. You generally do not like to be told what to do, so anything too structured or with too many rules is not for you. You want the freedom to do things your own way; you need to be able to express yourself without any pressure or constraint. A lesson for you is to learn to cope with structure and discipline, but any rules will need to make sense and not restrict you too much. You get bored very quickly and you like a challenge. You have a lot of physical energy and you hardly ever seem to get tired - but although you do need to 'walk off' or 'sweat out' stuff, be aware that you can burnout without even noticing. However, it is really important for you to incorporate some sort of physical activity into your daily life, otherwise any unused energy can increase your anxiety and assertiveness. You are goal-oriented and like to win or be first; you are usually very driven. Vigorous, active sports may suit you, or some activity where there is an atmosphere and element of competition - or at least where you can be better than everyone else! You need to feel in charge, or that you are a leader, and you need to test yourself by opposing someone else, so solo activities wouldn't suit you much unless it is something where you can compete against your own personal best. However, you need to be gently guided to see other points of view and contributions. You would possibly benefit from an athletics club where you can participate in lots of different sports, or a running club where you go on a new route each time (and you love races!). You may like a gym, where you can do a new routine each visit. You often do well at hockey, netball, football, boxing and wrestling. You would also like something strenuous such as jive dancing, and risky sports such as mountaineering or rock climbing also may appeal to you. You can also manifest your love of risk in speed, so you may like racing cars or motorbikes.

• Taurus

If you are Taurus, you need time to decide what you want to do. You can't have an activity sprung on you; you hate being forced or rushed into a decision or an action. You would benefit from physical exercise, but because you need to see things through to completion and always finish what you start, you should choose something you really enjoy; if you don't, you will tend to get bored and lose interest - and although you won't give it up, you just wouldn't be getting much out of it. You need to be sure that what you embark on is going to be right for you, as you find it difficult to change course once you have started something. You will need to think things through in your own time and commit to something when you feel ready. You can't be pushed into pro-gressing to more advanced activities either; you need to choose for yourself when to increase the difficulty. You are an amazing gardener and can create the most beautiful, verdant outdoor spaces, but this would need to involve 'physical' landscape gardening - things like digging, raking the gravel, hoeing the vegetables, redesigning etc. You don't like the pressure of having to hurry so you wouldn't particularly enjoy a gym or most team games. However, you need to try and social-ise with others sometimes, as you can occasion-ally hold negative judgements about yourself and rely on others to gently reassure you that these are false. Other than dancing and weightlifting (which you could possibly enjoy), you would be better off with outdoor pursuits. You can also do very well in something that requires stamina and endurance, like running marathons

● Gemini

If you are Gemini, you will always be busy and need a lot of variety in whatever you do. You need to be given freedom to choose from a wide range of activities, but you will probably need encour-agement to meet the requirements. Because of the duality in your nature, you have a need to decide between two or more courses of action. However, you are indecisive, so this can cause problems. You love travel and change and will probably hate doing one specific thing for any length of time.

You have an instinctive need to be always on the go, so physical exercise is a good way for you to release tension. To motivate yourself when you first start something physical, you could always use headphones and listen to music or podcasts, but reduce their use as soon as you can, as using these can reduce your chances of getting into flow. You must make sure that you don't commit yourself to anything that lasts for a long time, as you can change your mind often and get bored very quickly. Because your way of dealing with this is to drop whatever is boring you and move on to the next thing, you must aim to avoid anything too monotonous; like Aries, you need to do things that give you scope for different experiences. However, you don't particularly relish a challenge and if it is too difficult you will quickly give up and move on to something easier. Therefore, you need to gradually increase the level of difficulty to enable you to become more focused. You are a friendly and very active person who likes to get around, meet people, and have as many different experiences as possible, so being part of a group would suit you. You tend to enjoy 'light' sports such as tennis, fencing, badminton, table tennis or archery.

• Cancer

Because Cancer is a water sign, things have to 'feel' right before you can be interested enough to totally commit to anything. All water signs also absorb the emotional vibrations of wherever they are, so it is important that you are always in positive environments. You naturally tend to be less physically active than other signs, and in order to be active you must first motivate your mind. You need to think you can do it, then you will. You are prone to dream and drift, so you need to focus and channel your energy appropriately. Because of your innate tendency to be self-sufficient and to do things on your own, you will need encouragement to socialise or join in groups. In general, you dislike exercise, but you will benefit from being encouraged and guided by your peers. Friends can motivate you by playing down the 'exercise' part of any activity and presenting things as a challenge, as you respond well to physical challenges. Solo activities are not really for you; you need the encouragement of friends, although you can channel your physical energy into some solo things like housework or home repairs. You don't want to have to think for yourself all of the time, so anything guided by others, or that is easy to do or follow, will appeal to you. You like to have a structure within which you can operate. You are musical, so would probably enjoy dancing, and you also enjoy gardening (this needs to be 'physical' gardening such as weeding, digging or hoeing. This is actually a good way for you to get yourself active). Once you begin to see the results of your actions, your pride in your achievements will spur you on. You may be especially good at swimming or boxing, and you would probably enjoy archery and sailing. You might even find that you enjoy participating in something like paintball!

• Leo

If you are Leo, you are happiest when you are the centre of attention, having a good time and running everything. You need to enjoy what you do; you will become very stubborn if someone tries to get you to do something you're not really interested in. You certainly can't do anything dull or boring. However, you will also want to do what everyone else is doing, so you may find yourself following the trend of the week, even though you're not that interested in it. As well as organising everything, you will need to be the best at everything too, so it is important for you to find an activity where you can eventually excel. If you do something in which you can win a medal, you will get gold! You thrive on challenge, so, like Aries, you need an activity where there is an element of competition, or at least where you can be better than everyone else. (It is very advisable that Aries and Leo don't compete against each other!) You prefer structure in your activities, so something that has recognisable rules will appeal to you, but at the same time you will get rebellious if someone else tries to impose rules on you. You need to feel that you have the choice of what to do. You don't do very well alone, so ideally you need to be in a team (as long as you are in charge), and your pride will make you finish what you start and see things through to completion. If your enthusiasm gets dampened for any reason, you are unlikely to try again, so choose your activities wisely. Dancing, as well as swimming, running and jogging may appeal to you.

• Virgo

If you are Virgo, you have very high standards in everything you do, and if you can't do something well then you would rather not to do it at all. You prefer to get all the details about the activity you want to do and then break everything down into smaller steps so that you are very sure of what is involved. You love a routine, although you can sometimes get bogged down in detail and be a bit too literal, which can take some of the fun out of things. You are happier under the direction of others, rather than taking full responsibility. This means that you do well as part of a team, but you feel that everyone should put in as much effort in as you do, which sometimes causes you frustration. You are a perfectionist and are always subconsciously seeking precision in whatever you attempt, but you can be too hard on yourself. Therefore, being with others would be beneficial to you, as they can help you to put things in perspective. You can be a bit inhibited sometimes, so you probably wouldn't want to do anything which involves being the centre of attention, but you also like to be noticed and acknowledged. You will need time to think everything through before you take up something new, so don't let yourself be rushed into anything. However, you need to find something physical to do as you thrive on constant activity and have lots of nervous energy to burn, and active exercise will help with this. You should find it easy to motivate yourself to begin a physical activity as you are so aware of the benefits of health and fitness. Being an Earth sign (like Taurus), you are good at gardening (although in an exact, regimented sort of way), and you would also benefit from aerobics, walking and cycling. You love your pets, so walking the dog (if you have one) would be a very good activity for you to start with.

• Libra

If you are Libra, you are the most social sign, so you will not want to do anything by yourself. You will do best in a group or with an exercise partner, but you find it hard to make a decision or voice an opinion, so other people will be taking charge. However, remember that because it is important for you to appease other people, be careful not to agree to do something just to please them in order to be liked or to be popular. It is really important that you are in pleasant surroundings, as this impacts on your general feeling of well-being. You are not that keen on hard work, so anything too strenuous will put you off. You will need time to weigh up the pros and cons of anything before you commit to it, although once you do start something you tend to just want to finish it as quickly as possible. You are generally not bothered about being the best or coming first, so competitive team sports don't really appeal to you. In fact, you ideally need to avoid too much competitiveness, because if there is too much conflict around that you can't control, you tend to become anxious. You may sometimes find yourself avoiding physical activity, but you need to learn self-discipline, so getting into a routine is beneficial for you. Activities will need to be balanced, as that also has a positive effect on your well-being; activities which combine physical effort with periods of calm would appeal – something like tai chi, yoga or pilates, for example. Anything graceful will appeal to you; you enjoy dancing, which would fulfil you need for aesthetics and stability.

• Scorpio

If you are Scorpio, you need to be kept very busy and find plenty of outlets for your highly powered emotional energy. You will do nothing by halves – whatever you embark on, you will achieve it, but remember that you can sometimes become obsessive when you get very involved in something. You need to find an activity that demands continued, determined effort and intense concentration. It is important that you find the right activity, though, as you tend to do things to extremes - either all or nothing. You also don't give up once you have started something, as you have a tremendous drive to succeed. You would enjoy doing something with your friends, so some sort of social activity would benefit you more than doing something alone. You like a challenge, but you need frequent rewards and feedback that you are doing well, so something with a lot of stages that are readily achievable would be good for you. However, you like to 'do the impossible', so it can't appear to be too easy! You need, and enjoy, discipline, so team games and robust sports would be beneficial, but you would do better if the rules aren't too rigid and inflexible. It is important that you find a physical channel for your powerful energy. In your need to achieve, though, you can push others aside – this is not because you want to come first (like Aries and Leo), but because you need to feel you have personally succeeded. Swimming or boxing would be very beneficial for you. You might also find you enjoy something like caving or potholing.

● Sagittarius

If you are Sagittarius, you are always full of enthusiasm and will start new things with great excitement. This tends to lessen as the activity goes along and things get stuck in details, or the going gets a little tough, or it simply gets a little boring. It is the challenge of the initial problem that interests you; once you know what you are doing then you lose interest. You need to find something that has many levels of difficulty in order to keep your attention, otherwise you will continually start something new. You tend to like unusual activities, and you appear to be rebellious, but this is actually a case of rebelling against arbitrary restrictions - once rules are explained to you and you understand them, only then you can follow them. However, you tend to overlook details, so whatever you choose to do can't have too many constraints or be too complicated. You often over-extend yourself with too many activities, so you need to aim to concentrate on what you are doing and see it through to the end. Ideally, you shouldn't do something that is too strenuous, as you have a tendency to use up your energy too rapidly. It is important that you take regular intervals of rest so as to recuperate. Also remember that when you get bored you begin to feel tired, and if that happens you will need to find something different to do. You cannot cope with restrictive discipline and feel inhibited if you are too tied down. You do enjoy dancing, and you also like sports, but you shouldn't do anything too competitive or rough as you can be clumsy and may become injured playing contact sports. Water sports like sailing, swimming or surfing will appeal to you. You would benefit from doing calmer pursuits sometimes, as these can help you still your mind. You generally love large animals, especially horses, so horse riding is very beneficial to you, or engaging in equestrian activities such as polo, jumping or racing (but remember to be careful!). Being outdoors is very important for your well-being, so long walks appeal to you because they help you feel free, which is something you need to feel.

• Capricorn

If you are Capricorn, you need to know exactly what you are doing, and you like to examine all the pros and cons of anything you do in advance. You will probably have to try several activities before you settle on something you love, but you are also a creature of habit so will stick to one thing once you find it. You plan your every move in great detail, and nothing turns you from your course when your mind is made up. You don't like to give up, so you will always see things through to the end with amazing determination and perseverance. You are very ambitious and want to excel over others, so something that has recognisable progress is important to you. You would like something that encourages you to achieve your personal best. You have strong self-discipline and a lot of ambition – you want to achieve in whatever you do; and you don't like to think that you have been unsuccessful. You prefer activities that allow you to make steady progress; and encouragement and praise is essential in keeping you motivated. You generally need support from others before you embark on physical exercise. Respect and recognition is important to you. You would not like to be part of a team as you don't want of interfere in other people's activities or have them meddle in yours. Also, because you sometimes have a quiet character, you may find it hard to assert yourself in a group. However, it will benefit you to be around people, so an activity that lets you be with others, even if not competing against them, would be advantageous. You are good at athletics, and you do very well at rock climbing.

• Aquarius

Typically, Aquarius is a bit of a contradiction. You prefer not to be bound by schedules and rules but can easily adapt to them if you must - although you need the freedom to work through any rules or structures in your own way. You would benefit from having many different things to choose from, so something that involves variety would be good for you, especially since you don't like to feel restricted. You have the determination and persistence to keep to a task, but sometimes your energy level is relatively low, which causes you to drop projects before they are completed. You would probably prefer an unusual or individual activity! You generally have your own way of doing things and refuse to do anything the 'normal' way, preferring your own highly individualistic approach. You are indifferent to the opinions of others, so you tend to do exactly what you want to, regardless of peer pressure or what is currently popular. You won't be interested in anything that is suggested to you - you need to choose what you do for yourself. You do your best in groups or teams, even though you may maintain a bit of distance. You hate anything boring and repetitive - the more extraordinary the better! Something like goat yoga would probably attract you! Learning how to fly a light aircraft may also appeal to you, and it also fulfils your need for individuality. Whatever you choose to do, it needs to be able to channel your excess mental energy; it needs to exercise your brain as well as your body.

• Pisces

If you are Pisces, as a Water sign, things have to 'feel' right before you can do them. You also absorb the emotional vibrations of wherever you are and whoever you are with, so it is important that you are always in positive environments and around uplifting people. You tend to just accept the situation, rather than trying to alter or control it. You lack a strong desire to work or to push yourself into doing anything that takes a lot of strength, discipline or routine; you struggle with any form of enforced structure or schedules. Although you can appear to be very determined on the outside, underneath, inner doubts are brewing. This insecurity causes you to need reassurance from others, so activities that involve others are important for you. You need to be around other people, so you need activities that are done in groups, but they must be groups in which you feel relaxed. You need regular periods of rest away from the every-day world to recharge your fluctuating energies. You do need fun, though, so anything that can lift your mood is beneficial. Activities that balance your sensitive energies will help you become more grounded. You are not keen on sports; as such, you would prefer things like ballet or skating, both of which would benefit you. Different forms of dance may also appeal to you. Whatever you choose, it needs to be a source of inspiration so you can identify with what you do. You may enjoy swimming, especially in the sea.

Obviously, this is not an exhaustive list and we won't necessarily show or feel all of the qualities detailed in our sign. Remember what we said before: all the planets in our chart can affect us, not just the Sun sign.

For example, I am a very typical Aries. I am impulsive and enthusiastic; I get bored very quickly and love variety, and I've lost count of the number of things I have started then given up when I moved on to something else. But I don't like sports at all. In fact, other than walking and dancing, I dislike all forms of exercise – not like a typical Aries. However, as well as having the Sun in Aries, I have the Moon in Cancer, and Cancers don't generally like physical exercise much at all! You may find you love to do something I have suggested for a different Sun sign to yours – you might love horses and horse riding for example, but you are not Sagittarius. However, if I looked at your chart, I would find that you almost certainly have Sagittarius or Jupiter (the planet that is the ruler of Sagittarius) somewhere significant. Use the attributes of the signs to guide you towards what is likely to suit you; if you like to be part of a team, it could be in a rowing club, volleyball, rounders, cricket - there are so many more options than I have listed. The ones I have specifically mentioned are recommended for those particular signs, but they are not the only possibilities. Whatever brings you flow experiences is good. The more you experience flow then the easier you will find the other mindful practice methods.

Creative Activities

Creative activities – where we are using our imagination and inspiration to make something new or produce our own version of something – is another way of having flow experiences. Creativity is having original ideas and being able to express them. There are many ways we can be creative, and although some people may appear to be more creative than others, everyone is able to produce something original.

Before we look at how the signs prefer to manifest their creativity, let's run through some of the choices available to us.

* Drawing
This is a good pastime for signs that like to be ac-

tive or use their hands, and it can be anything from a beautifully sketched canvas to a series of swirls where you have kept your pencil on the page and drawn a pattern of random squiggles (you can get colouring pages like this already drawn, but it is more fun to draw your own). You can doodle or draw a 'pattern' by just scribbling without even really thinking about it, or by repeating symbols across a page (using the astrology glyphs or healing symbols is enlightening),or drawing a series of shapes. You can draw a picture; it doesn't matter how good it is or isn't - remember, in flow we lose our self-consciousness. You can draw your own mandala or labyrinth (details on these later). You could also create patterns with an old Spirograph drawing tool, which create beautiful mandala-like patterns.

You can recreate some of the activities you did as a child – colour a piece of paper all over with wax crayons in lots of different colours, and then cover the whole page with black wax crayon. You can then scratch off the black wax to reveal lines of different colours. You would experience flow both in the initial colouring and then in scratching the lines!

An interesting drawing exercise is to get a sheet of plain paper and draw an outdoor scene which must include a tree. You can colour it in if you like. Do this now, and I'll explain the next steps later in the book!

* Colouring

You can colour in your own doodles, patterns or drawings, or use colouring books – there are so many available now, you will be able to find a topic that appeals to you. You can colour mandalas and labyrinths (your own or pre-drawn ones). Colouring is a great way to experience flow. It is especially helpful if you use your non-writing hand to colour in, as this encourages you to use different neural pathways in your brain and strengthens the connections, even encouraging the growth of new neurons. Although it feels odd initially, the more you practise colouring (or doing other things) with your non-dominant hand, the more benefits you will experience and the easier you will find it to practise mindfulness.

* Painting

As with drawing, you can paint a picture – using watercolours, oils or acrylics, you can splodge paint onto paper, or you can doodle with a paintbrush. You can paint pre-drawn pictures instead of colouring them, or you can paint your doodles or mandalas and labyrinths if you prefer that to colouring.

* Writing

Writing is another good way of having flow experiences. I have lost count of the number of times I have experienced flow while writing this book! Everyone can write, it doesn't have to be a story or a poem although, of course, they are very good for encouraging flow.. You can write a letter to someone – this can be an actual 'letter' that you post. Alternatively, you can write a 'letter' if you have something you want to say to somebody but are not sure you can (or want to). This is a good thing to do as you can get all your thoughts and feelings out on paper and then burn it. This has a very therapeutic effect and can help you come to terms with your emotions. You can also just write down your thoughts as they occur to you, keep a dream journal or a diary, or write a gratitude list (a very good thing to get into the habit of doing – list as many things as you can that you are grateful for).

* Art using different materials

This is where you are creative using different mediums such as designing mosaics or jewellery, making things with resin, or using clay (sculpting and pottery) or wood (wood carving or making driftwood models). All of these tactile methods encourage flow experiences.

* Music

Another creative area is music, and this is very good at providing flow experiences. Music is creative when you play an instrument or compose music. Learning to play a musical instrument has amazing benefits to the brain (it increases neuron growth and plasticity) and is a very good way of getting into mindfulness.

* Drama

Joining a drama group, acting or entertaining others in some way can help you get into flow.

Recreational Activities

Recreational activities are also called hobbies - things we like to do in our spare time. If we really enjoy what we do and challenge ourselves enough, we can experience flow. There can be a blur in the boundary between creative and recreational activities, but hopefully we can appreciate the subtle difference. Hobbies are sometimes called pastimes or interests, but, really, they are (or can be) so much more than that. We should truly love what we do; if we have a hobby but don't love it (or experience flow), then we should find a new one. We don't want to spend our precious time doing something that isn't bringing us any benefits.

A recreational activity can be something that we do alone or with someone else, and it can be indoors or outdoors. There are so many things we could do that it is impossible to name them all. However, here are some ideas to get us started:

* Reading

It is easy to experience flow when reading for pleasure -very often people are so engrossed in their book that they don't hear you speak to them, for example. You will need to find the level of book that encourages flow; books that require a lot of concentration, such as text books, can sometimes result in flow, although books you are made to read as part of a course syllabus are unlikely to result in flow experiences.

* Cooking
Concentrating on following a recipe, chopping, mixing, whisking, blending stirring and combining the ingredients etc. can all help to you experience flow.

* Singing
Singing along to your favourite songs in the privacy of your own home or in the car, or joining a choir - it doesn't matter where you sing, the action of focusing on the music and concentrating on the words will bring flow.

* Listening to music
Flow is usually experienced when listening to classical or relaxing music, or if you are listening to music to sing along to it. Listening to specific genres of music can often result in flow, especially if you love that style. Commercial 'pop' songs don't usually bring flow, although they can sometimes.

* Origami or Quilling
The act of concentrating on folding the paper and following the instructions aids flow. This is easy to make more challenging too, as the designs can get more and more complex as you improve your

technique.

* Jigsaws

Searching for jigsaw pieces and then finding where to put them focuses your mind and encourages flow. Again, you can do whatever level of jigsaw is a challenge for you.

* Card Games

Solo games like solitaire, or social games like bridge or poker can bring flow experiences. This is due to the concentration you need to give to the tactics or the attentiveness on the cards themselves.

* Games

Activities like chess, or other games such as scrabble or backgammon, can give you fairly intense flow experiences. These are games that you need to concentrate on or that have a strategy, but any game has the potential to bring flow – even playing 'Hungry Hippo' with the kids may possibly count!

* Sewing and Dressmaking

The act of laying out the material, cutting out a pattern, pinning, tacking, machining, hand sewing - all of these things can give you flow experiences.

* Knitting or Crochet

The rhythmic action of moving the needle(s) combined with working the wool is good for flow.

When you get very accomplished, you may need to increase the complexity of the pattern, or there is the risk that you will start to do it on autopilot.

* Embroidery, Tapestry or Cross-stitch

Again, handling the cottons and rhythmically moving the needle, as well as focusing on where you are putting the stitches, can bring flow.

* Sudoku

This is good for people who enjoy maths; the concentration on the pattern of the numbers encourages flow.

* Crosswords, Logic Puzzles or Wordsearch

These types of activities are good for people who like language and communication; having to focus on the letters and words will bring flow, unless it is too easy for you. Remember to keep challenging yourself.

* Flower Arranging

Choosing the flowers, deciding on the colours, cutting the stems, arranging them in the vase - all of these things can bring flow. Usually you need to be arranging more than one bunch of flowers though!

* Light Gardening

Activities like dead-heading, picking flowers, tying up climbing plants - spending time outdoors in a space you love is very beneficial and encourages flow experiences.

You will automatically experience flow when you become proficient at an activity and can do it without really thinking about the specifics. Remember, though, that it needs to be challenging enough so that you have to focus on it, and not start getting bored and letting your mind wander. However, don't let the fact that you need to have mastered something put you off even starting it. It takes time to become really good at something – some studies say it takes 10,000 hours of practise! So even if you are not very good at playing that new musical instrument you have just bought, keep practising and you will get better and better, ultimately leading to flow experiences. Unless you really don't like something, try not to give up just because you think you can't do it. If you know that you do tend to give up easily then start with something simple and work up to harder things, or set yourself mini goals to achieve which will keep you motivated. Baby steps are the way forward! Doing something that helps you to experience flow will make you happier and pave the way for other mindfulness practices. It cannot be over-emphasised how important it is, and it is so easy to do that there is no excuse not to start immediately.

Did you draw the outdoor scene from earlier? Notice how empty or full the picture is. What colours did you use? The scene represents your life and the tree represents you. Knowing this, what does your drawing say about how you feel about your environment and yourself? How important do you feel in the scheme of things? Understanding how you feel now will help you determine where to direct your energies to develop yourself and your mindfulness.

Astrology Signs and Creative/ Recreational Activities

Now we can look at the astrology signs and their predisposition towards creative and recreational activities, but remember that, as I have mentioned before, we won't necessarily show or feel all of the qualities detailed in our sign, as all of the planets in our chart can affect us, not just the Sun sign. You may find you love to do something I have suggested for a different Sun sign to yours, and that's fine – if I looked at your chart, you would most likely have that sign, or the planet that rules the sign, prominent. Try as many different activities as you can; there may be something you haven't previously thought of which you end up absolutely loving! And remember to be open-minded, as some aspects of your sign may be lessons you need to learn.

• Aries

If you are Aries, you are very creative and always come up with new ideas. You like activities you have devised yourself and won't want to do anything involving too much detail, or anything that takes too long to complete. Your thoughts bound around instead of following a logical progression (that would be much too boring!), so you need something flexible that can be picked up and then discarded as your mood takes you. Remember, though, if you cannot overcome this basic tendency to dabble shallowly in many activities, you will not master any skill completely. You don't often finish things, so you should be discouraged from spending out a lot of money on equipment or materials, as you won't use them for long. It would be beneficial for you to have two or three different hobbies on the go at the same time, that you can dip in and out of at will, to alleviate your inevitable boredom. Try and ensure that at least one hobby is 'active' so that you can channel your energy productively. If you do activities with others, in a group for example, you will want to do better than everyone else, and if there are competitions you would like to win. You could be very a good sculptor and also be good at wood carving (you may excel at things that involve sharp tools). You probably also love reading, and again will probably have several books on the go at once. You may also show writing ability – possibly in the form of correspondence (your emails will be excellent!). Whatever you do, you need the freedom to express yourself without any pressure or restriction; you will rebel at the first hint of discipline.

• Taurus

If you are Taurus, you need to see the point of the things that you do, so you won't start something just for the sake of it; you will want it to have a purpose, as you appreciate practicality. You do not make decisions in a hurry (so others need to be prepared to wait while you determine what to do) and cannot work in a hurry, but once your mind is made up you will work patiently until your task is finished. You do sometimes work at a slower pace than some people, and probably find it difficult to change direction halfway through. You can be very obstinate! You need to learn adaptability and be encouraged to try different things, otherwise you will stick to one thing and therefore not stretch yourself. You need to be shaken up a bit, otherwise you may tend to continue along without changing anything in your life. You like to work with your hands and build things (you are very practical), and you appreciate beauty – you would make a good jeweller. You are probably good at sculpting and pottery; you excel at crafting in general. You may have a talent for art and could be very drawn to music; you are probably a very good singer. You love nature and gardens, so as well as the 'heavy' landscape-type gardening, you enjoy (and are good at) growing things generally – you will benefit from having lots of indoor plants. You won't want to travel very far, so need to find activities which are close by or done at home.

• Gemini

If you are Gemini, you love being involved in several things at once and are likely to have many projects on the go at the same time. You do need to learn to control your energy and your mind, otherwise you will flit about not settling to anything. Like Aries, you don't often finish things, so you should be discouraged from spending out a lot of money on equipment or materials, as you won't use them for long. You don't like going too deeply into anything and have a tendency to skim the surface, so you need to find creative activities that you can do without too much 'learning' first. You need activities with structure though, or you will fritter away your energy. You would get a lot of benefit from learning a musical instrument, but as you will want to try several different ones, borrow rather than purchase! You are also a good writer, so have a go at this in any form – book, poetry, diary – and you can be good with your hands, so most creative pursuits would be interesting to you (albeit briefly!). You are a lively talker, fond of arguments and discussions, and you can express your views easily, so some form of debating society would be good for you. Because you can absorb information quickly, you can sometimes give the impression of being better informed than you really are. You generally prefer intellectual games or quizzes, rather than physical activities. Anything that provides you with an intellectual challenge will benefit you; you are excellent at all word games, e.g. scrabble. You are good at languages and enjoy working on computers. You may also enjoy travelling, particularly shorter journeys. You like to talk about your experiences, so keeping a blog or similar would benefit you.

• Cancer

If you are Cancer, your heart must be in a project fully before you can commit to it, so you must completely connect with what you do. You need to be in calm surroundings before you can relax enough to allow yourself to be creative. You have a good imagination and can be good at writing; you would enjoy something like keeping a diary or history of your dreams, or your thoughts and feelings regarding your day-to-day happenings. What you choose to do depends on your mood to an unusual degree, but you will be drawn to things like art, poetry, music, or mythology. It would be useful if you have several options to choose from, so that you can vary what you do according to how you feel. Playing a musical instrument would also be good for you. You may have a strong tendency to live in the past, and you love history and your family, so you would probably enjoy researching your family tree, making family photo albums, restoring antiques, or collecting old family memorabilia. You need to nurture others and your home-making skills are excellent; you are probably a good cook and you can make the best of your surroundings, so things like baking appeal to you, or making things that can be used by other people. You are also drawn to water so would benefit from spending time around the sea, lakes or rivers, or even a garden pond. You also get a lot of pleasure from being with animals, especially dogs.

● Leo

If you are Leo, you are very creative and artistic, but you tend to lack an eye for detail, so you should avoid anything too intricate. However, you have big ideas and need to do something fairly easy that gives you impressive results without too much effort. You can't do anything you find dull or boring. You are likely to develop your creative and artistic talents in all directions and you must have something of your own, something innovative, that you can develop according to your own vision. You would be good at designing jewellery. Whatever you do, you do it in a unique, dramatic, individual way. You like to put your own personal stamp on it. You are very dramatic and would probably benefit from doing something theatre related, such as a drama group or acting (as long as you take the lead!). You may have a fondness for children and the ability to bring out the best in them, so doing something with, or for, children could be beneficial. You like to be surrounded by light and life and have an interest in health and fitness. You tend to enjoy activities that are good for your health, so aim to do things outdoors, if possible, or things that benefit your wellbeing, such as walking or gardening. Due to your tendency to enjoy being a leader, you often find that competition is a great way to relieve stress and tension. You like to take the lead in planning activities, and once a new project is started you are determined to see it finished. You have a natural store of energy and your friends may have trouble keeping up with your zest for work and fun.

• Virgo

If you are Virgo, you are very careful in everything you do and love to do things involving intricate detail. You like to achieve and will worry about starting something if you're not sure you can do it to your own high standards. You may also struggle in choosing a hobby; you are indecisive, or, having made a decision, you often look back and worry if you've done the right thing. Hidden beneath your quiet and modest surface, however, is a deep-seated desire for emotional expression of an intensely dramatic nature. The emotional side of your nature really needs to find freedom of expression. Therefore, if you participate in the Arts, particularly theatre, you will find immense happiness and release in this outlet for your inner self. Anything that requires you to learn elaborate techniques that demand a lot of skill will interest you. It may even be something that you do with your hands, as long as it is complicated enough – you may like intricate construction kits, for example. Although you are not particularly artistically inclined, you possess a shrewd eye for form and design. You want to do it all, and in your own way, rather than depending on someone else to do their share. You do like to be active and you have a psychological need to do healthy things most of the time, so activities like gardening may be more appealing to you than artistic pursuits. However, you would be good at painting and dress-making; as you have a talent for crafting. You learn easily and are well suited for research, so you may enjoy problem solving, or computer adventure games. You love things that challenge your brain. You probably also enjoy reading, too. You have remarkable powers of observation and find it easy to formulate ideas into writing. Anything involving sorting or classifying something would appeal to you. You also get a lot of satisfaction from animals (especially small animals, particularly cats), so you would enjoy tailoring your creativity towards them - making mazes out of boxes, for example. It is very important for your well-being that you have a quiet period each day in order to rest your active mind, so once you get into flow and begin mindfulness you will see the benefits very quickly.

● Libra

If you are Libra, you have an elegant style and good taste, but you need congenial surroundings; you are not good at concentrating if you feel you are in unpleasant conditions. You do better as part of a group, so would benefit from classes of some sort. However, you are fairly easy-going and will usually give way to stronger personalities, so you must be careful that you are not pushed into doing something you don't really want to do, as you won't be able to completely involve yourself in something unless you really enjoy it. However, unless the activity is simple (colouring, for example), you work best together with a partner who is prepared to take the main share of responsibility and decisions. You are flexible and willing to listen to all sides of an issue. This may lead to uncertainty and indecision, though, because sometimes you cannot make up your mind as to which side has the most merit. Your thinking process works by means of comparing things and finding analogies - this is when you are at your best. You love being surrounded by nice things, and tend to be artistically inclined, and have a good sense of colour and arrangement; everything from flower arranging to interior design is within your range of talents. You may also develop a taste for art and literature. You are very imaginative, but you need to learn to control this a bit or you tend to get carried away. Your natural creativity could lead you to participate in singing, dancing, drawing, writing, sewing, decorating, and music (you will do well in a band or orchestra, or writing music). You also enjoy the seclusion of places of beauty.

• Scorpio

If you are Scorpio, when you can find a creative outlet for your tremendous inner strength, you can achieve amazing things. You are very resolute and once you make up your mind about an activity it is unlikely to change; you will be determined to achieve the objectives you set for yourself. You take great pride in your achievements and will want to know everything about the creative activity you are doing, yet if you find out any tips or shortcuts, you will keep them a secret! You would prefer to learn a new skill by hands-on practise or direct experience rather than learning from a book or being taught by someone else. You can't do something for the sake of it, you need to do something that rouses your passion and then you can focus completely on what you are doing. (Of all the signs, Scorpio has the ability to become completely immersed in what they do, and so can experience flow easily.). You would benefit from being near or on water, or in researching something; you have to get to the bottom of whatever it is that interests you. You love discovering and analysing – logic problems often suit you, and you enjoy reading mysteries or detective books, or participating in discussion groups. You have mechanical ability and work well with your hands, so you are good at making detailed models. Your intensity of emotion and feeling is a good quality if you are drawn to participate in theatre or acting activities; your flair for melodrama could be developed to good use in theatrical productions.

● Sagittarius

If you are Sagittarius you need to feel free and uncommitted and cannot bear to be tied down to people or situations, so ideally you need to avoid complicated and costly long-term memberships to things. You become rebellious and militant when frustrated, so you need to feel in control of what you do. You need the freedom to do it, or not to do it, as you choose. As long as instructions are explained to you so that you can understand them, you are happy to follow them; you need to feel that something will agree with you before you start. You have a quick, keen mind, but you struggle to concentrate, tending to work in fits and starts, and often leaving things unfinished. You have a constant need for intellectual challenge and never stop learning things. You are generally unconcerned about the results of what you do and would prefer to avoid doing anything that involves too much detail, as you would rather see the bigger picture. However, you take pride in your achievements once you finish something.

You tend to be clumsy with material things, so could struggle with using substances like clay or wood. You are also quite accident prone, so that is another reason to avoid sharp tools! You are good at languages and can be interested in foreign cultures or religions; you also love reading and studying and probably have writing ability. You love being outdoors, and a good deal of travel is possible. You enjoy games and competitions, and joining a large group or organisation could help to expand you personally.

• Capricorn

If you are Capricorn, you generally tend to be very practical and probably ask what the point of something is before you embark on it. Like Taurus, you need to see the relevance of the things that you do, so you won't start something just for the sake of it; you will want it to have a purpose. You have a fear of failure so will need to know that you can accomplish what you set out to do, and you have the patience to complete the work necessary to achieve your ideas. You are capable of working long hours with focused concentration and attention on whatever interests you, so be aware of this and don't overtax yourself. You may find that you need to try several different activities before you settle on the one or two that you then continue with. You will take what you do seriously, and you do not like to be teased by others. You enjoy time alone, so need to find something to do that doesn't involve other people too much. However, being a member of a club or organised group could provide contacts that may prove valuable in furthering your long-range interests. Although you may not have out-standing artistic talents, you are musical and can easily learn a musical instrument; you also love listening to music. Serious-minded and studious, you enjoy quiet time alone for thinking or read-ing – you are a voracious reader. You are also good at science and maths - you're logical and have an excellent memory. Something like Sudoku would be good for you. You also like archaeology; maybe this can be channelled into a 'Fossil (or Dinosaur) Dig' kit or similar, or you can join a local archae-ology group.

• Aquarius

If you are Aquarius, you generally get along well with your companions, but there are times when you need periods of quiet and solitude. You like to spend time in societies and group activities, especially those based upon a common interest, but you also like to do your own thing within the group. You are very imaginative and original and tend not to care what others think, and you usually find controversial discussions stimulat-ing. You are a bit of an enigma – modern in out-look but fixed in opinion. You are not likely to stay interested in anything that becomes routine or dull, and a congenial atmosphere is important to you. Doing things with highly technical inventions or systems – such as computers – would be an area where you can do well. However, you will do everything your own way and not pay attention to the 'proper' way of doing something. You're often curious about foreign cultures and this can lead to doing old things in new ways. Your interests generally need to challenge your intellectual capabilities, and you will benefit from having a lot of different things to choose from. Whatever you do will undoubtedly tend towards the slightly eccentric and unpredictable. You often react strongly against any restrictions or limitations imposed upon you, since your freedom is very important to you. You have a flair for artistic activities, and music ability is likely; you will benefit from learning a musical instrument, and it will probably be something unusual. You may enjoy scientific things, particularly chemistry, and you would probably enjoy astronomy and archaeology. Anthropology could also appeal to you.

• Pisces

If you are Pisces, you have a wonderful imagination and you love to spend time daydreaming and making up fantasies, for you can see the world in ways that are hidden from many others. You need to get a balance with this, though, and not use it to escape from reality, and you need to be encouraged to have fun and be playful. You don't like too much discipline or too many restrictions so will need to find something that allows you to drift along at your own pace. Sometimes it is difficult for you to choose what to do, because your emotions influence your thinking so much. You like to achieve things on your own, without any formal training or plan, and it is not easy for you to conform. Conventional 'book' learning may not be your area of strength, yet you can absorb knowledge in the most remarkable ways if you are interested in the subject area. Many forms of art and music may appeal to you and you are good at, and enjoy, painting. You generally enjoy drama and acting because it gives you the opportunity to be someone else. You are also good at comedy mime, and generally have a talent for entertaining others – you would be good at doing sleight of hand magic. Creative pursuits interest you, particularly the writing of poems, plays, novels and mystery stories, should you decide to explore this possibility. You are also drawn to languages and religion, although this is not in a formal sense. You don't mind working alone or in smaller spaces and you enjoy being with one or two special people rather than participating in group activities.

In discussing hobbies and activities that will benefit the astrology signs, you may find that you already do that particular thing, or you hate what is suggested, or you like an activity recommended for a different sign to your own. That's all fine;

remember, there are lots of influences on a natal chart, not just the Sun sign, so it may be that you are reflecting your Moon sign, or your Ascendant. It doesn't matter! What is important is that you experience flow, become happier and eventually develop your ability to be mindful.

Find an activity that you enjoy, do it as often as you can, and eventually you will experience flow; this is the first step towards practising mindfulness.

Flow and Technology

There has been a lot of research into the types of activities which give people flow, and although we don't always know exactly what sort of activities will bring us flow experiences, we do know the sorts of activities that won't; flow is a rare occurrence in activities such as housework, idling and resting.

Many people find they have flow-like experiences when using technology; sometimes these are actual flow experiences, but very often they are not! For example, many people can sit for hours watching TV without noticing how much time has passed, but they are not being mindful; it is more they are acting on autopilot. Remember, it is not just a balance between challenge and skill that is required for flow, but rather both have to be stretched. In watching television, the low skill matches the low challenge, which usually results in apathy or boredom.

However, flow is often experienced when people play video games; the emergence of flow during gaming is in part due to the balance between the ability of the player and the difficulty of the game, concentration, direct feedback, clear goals, and control over the activity. There was even a trial video game called 'Flow' based on the Flow Theory; the game automatically adjusted its difficulty and reactions based on the actions (skill of the player. Through this personalised challenge/skill balance, less skilled players reported an increase in control over the gameplay that was necessary to feel more immersed in the game and to achieve flow.

Generally, though, technology is a massive distraction, and many apps - even meditation apps - can function in ways that take your attention away from direct experiences. Things like phones and laptops constantly pull at our attention, and although we seem immersed when scrolling through Facebook etc., we are not genuinely experiencing flow.

Even though flow can be experienced while performing a variety of technology-based tasks (ranging from word processing, programming, visual design, playing games and online searches), we should not solely rely on these things for all of our flow experiences. We need to consciously choose to participate in other activities that we also enjoy. It would be wise for everyone to have a digital detox every now and then. We should all schedule some deliberate time into our life where we don't use any technology at all. This could be a few hours per day or a half day per week, or whatever suits our needs best or more appropriately.

If you use digital devices a lot, when you first have a break from them you may feel anxiety and a sense of disconnection or boredom. These are symptoms of being mentally over-stimulated. Just accept these feelings and try very hard to resist the urge to reach for the nearest device. If you find this very hard, you should aim to spend a short time away from technology and build it up gradually.

2. Being A Fly on the Wall

The second way to practise mindfulness techniques is by being a fly on the wall. This is another way of explaining the technique of stepping outside the boundary of our Ego, so that we can look at ourselves objectively. Remember from earlier, the 'real you' generally lives in our subconscious mind and the conscious mind is run by our Ego.

Imagine that you are given the opportunity to be a fly on the wall for any event from the past. Whatever the event you choose, the idea of being a fly on the wall is that you are a disinterested observer – not an 'uninterested' observer, but a 'disinterested' one. There's an interesting difference between being uninterested and disinterested! Uninterested is what it sounds like: it means being bored and not interested. Disinterested means being unbiased. Therefore, you can be a disinterestedly interested observer of something, which is what you are when you're a fly on the wall for an event that you think is significant.

As a fly on the wall, you would want to merely observe whatever was going on in the past without adding or taking away anything from it. That is, you wouldn't want to attract attention to yourself, and you wouldn't want to change whatever was going on either. In fact, even if you wanted to change something, you would know that as a fly on the wall you don't have the power to change or control things. You simply have to accept whatever was going on and just take the opportunity to witness the significant event unfolding in front of your eyes.

Now, imagine that instead of being a fly on the wall for an external significant event you are instead a fly on the wall in your head, watching what you are thinking and feeling right now. As the fly on the wall for an external event, you couldn't change what was happening or what you were observing. But, as a fly on the wall in your head, you could change what was happening. For example, if your Ego had a thought, "I am a such a pig for eating a whole bar of chocolate by myself" you could change that thought and tell yourself, "I'm not a pig, I am going through a bad time and finding comfort". You can control your thoughts and thus discover the beginnings of mindfulness, although this does take a lot of practise!

It's really difficult not to let our mind wander when we're feeling stressed or negative because in those situations we end up doing something called 'ruminating'. We start to build on the negative feelings which soon spiral out of control. For example, if you just got shouted at by your boss, you may think that he's unfair and he always shouts at you. This thought might, in turn, trigger thoughts of how you're probably going to lose your job soon, since the company's looking to make people redundant, and so on. It's important to note that when we ruminate, we're not being mindful, although it might seem as though we're being in the present moment.

Being mindful does mean focusing on whatever we're experiencing at the present moment. So, for instance, if our boss has just shouted at us, and we feel upset, being mindful means to experience those feelings. What does it feel like to be upset, without thinking other thoughts that either intensify or mitigate this feeling? Remember that being mindful is totally focusing on whatever it is that we're feeling or thinking, not running away from it, accepting it fully, and embracing it, even. Mindfulness means not trying to regulate your thoughts or your feelings. In fact, what we're trying to do is the opposite of controlling our thoughts and feelings. What we're trying to do is merely observe what's going on without passing judgement.

Imagine you suddenly have a thought. "Oh no, it's late. I need to pick up my son from school." Usually when we have such a thought, we let it determine the next thought, which could be something like, "I should try to be a little more organised. I never do things on time." Which in turn could trigger an emotion such as guilt and perhaps that might trigger an action of rushing to the car. On the way to the car, you might pick up a treat for your son to appease him, just in case he's upset about you being late. Let's look at what's going on in this example. A thought that you might be late evokes another thought that you're bad at time management, which in turn triggers an emotion, guilt, which in turn triggers the action of rushing to your car, and the goal of trying appease your son. So, basically, the original thought has triggered a web of consequences that evoke thoughts and emotions and actions. Almost every thought that we have does this. We normally live in a web that our thoughts, emotions and actions weave for us; in other words, our Ego usually dictates how we feel and what we do.

Another way to think about this is to imagine a drop of water falling into a pond, causing ripples. The droplet falling into the pond is our initial thought, and our sensations and emotions. The next ripple is the thought that comes next, and the outer ripples are the subsequent thoughts that develop from there. Thoughts, emotions and actions will carry on generating further thoughts, emotions and actions unless we find a way to direct our attention somewhere else. If when our boss shouts at us, we react in a way that's healthy, then it's not too bad. But, unfortunately, most of us don't react in a healthy way to many of the events and experiences that life throws at us. One way to break the cycle is to step outside the boundary of the Ego - become a fly on the wall in our head.

As a fly on the wall in our head, we'd be aware of all the thoughts, emotions and actions that we were experiencing. And because we're a disinterested fly, we wouldn't want to change any of them. We'd merely be observing and noting what is going on, but without commenting or judging anything. If we successfully manage to do this, what we would discover is that the pace of thoughts, emotions and actions that are triggered slows down. The reason this happens is that when we're a fly on the wall, we put some distance between ourselves and what's going on, and this distance lowers the intensity of our emotional reactions to the other parts of the web – the actions and thoughts.

When the intensity of our emotional reactions is lower, the action tendencies and thoughts also decrease in intensity. So as a result, the whole system slowly calms down. This calmness will naturally bring about two important consequences.

First, we will feel more tranquil, or less stressed. There are a lot of studies on mindfulness that have shown that the practice of mindfulness lowers stress. The second consequence is that you will develop something called 'response flexibility'. We will be able to notice exactly when and which emotion triggered a particular thought. By contrast, if we're not a fly on the wall, but rather a fly that's caught in the web, you will not be able to discern the cause and relationship in the chain of events. This ability to discern what triggers what, and when, will give you the ability to step in, if we choose to, to make a more conscious decision. That is, rather than being helplessly tangled in the web when we're thinking our Ego's thoughts or behaving in certain conditioned ways, we'll be able to choose how we react to a particular stimulus. Therefore, the more we practice merely observing what's going on without judging or commenting on it - which is what mindfulness is about - the better we become at it.

Although the idea of being a fly on the wall in our head (or stepping out of the boundary of our Ego) might seem like we're putting a distance between ourselves and what's going on in our head, what we're actually attempting to do is to get into touch with the reality of the moment, rather than trying to change what's going on, which is what takes us away from the moment.

Think about what happens normally, when you're

not being a fly on the wall or you're not being mindful – you're caught up in the web of your thoughts, actions and emotions. This usually means that you are thrown around various parts of the web. Your boss shouting at you takes us to a previous time that he might have shouted at you and then to other bosses who have shouted at you before. That leads you to think of your parents who used to shout at you, which in turn leads you to think about how you are never going succeed in life, which leads you to all the dreams that you might have had when you were a child and so on. So, in other words, as a fly stuck in the web, you'd be lurching wildly from the present, your boss shouting, to the past, your ex-bosses and your parents shouting, back to the present (I'm never going to succeed), to the future (dreams for the future), etc. As you can see from this example, being a fly in the web involves a lot of time travel. By contrast, as a fly on the wall in your head, you're firmly rooted in the present. You're observing what's going on right now in your head. Your thoughts, actions and emotions may be doing some time traveling but you are in the present, and if you manage to stay in the present (which means that you don't fly off the wall and into the web) you will discover that these thoughts, actions and emotions will also come back to the present. When this happens, a third consequence follows, which is that you'll get more in touch with your senses. That is, you spend less time in your head, in the web of your mind, and more time in your body. You're thinking more through your senses than you otherwise would.

Astrology Signs and Being a Fly on the Wall

Obviously, we are all going to find our own way to practise being a fly on the wall in our heads, but the different signs can help us in our approach to it.

If you are a Fire Sign (Aries, Leo and Sagittarius), your basic approach is one of spontaneous action. You will approach this new thing with great enthusiasm, but your emotional response is so quick that you will struggle to remain a disinterested observer. You will need to practise using a lot of very small steps in order to build up any detachment and distance from your thoughts, actions and emotions. Being so impulsive, you will be reacting before there is even time for the fly to observe what is going on! Try and aim for microseconds of distance initially (even just thinking about being a fly on the wall is a start for you). When a situation occurs that provokes an emotional reaction from you, just think, 'I should be a fly now', and aim to count to ten before you do or say anything. If you can acknowledge, 'I am caught in my web of thoughts, actions and emotions' before you react, you will find it easier and easier to maintain this thought and get more control of your emotions and actions. You will remain motivated by assessing what you are actually achieving against what you aim to achieve – this will spur you on to keep practising. Aries: your basic response is enthusiastic but undirected so keep focusing on your goals; Leo: you will get creative with your approach to this, and you will make more progress once you have had some success; Sagittarius: you will make the most progress by exploring all of the possibilities available to you.

If you are an Earth Sign (Taurus, Virgo and Capricorn), your basic approach is one of practicality and orderliness. You are a complete contrast to the Fire Signs in that you excel in common-sense but you can sometimes lack enthusiasm. Because you can become absorbed in practical things, you have a tendency to only believe what can be perceived with your five senses. You will often find yourself focusing on what actually is, rather than speculating on what might be, so you can sometimes struggle to see the point of things that are vague or undefined, like being a fly on the wall in your head. A lot of the mindfulness techniques may seem a bit unrealistic to you initially, so you will need to suspend your scepticism and give it all a try. Once you start, you will be very good at distancing yourself from your Ego, as emotionally you are deeply rooted and slower to change, so you will find that you are generally slower at getting caught in the web in the first place. You will remain motivated by assessing the external facts – what are you experiencing through your senses? When you know where you are then you can structure where you want to be. Taurus: you will have the most practical approach and will be very structured in the methods you use; Virgo: you will make most progress by using a measured analysis determining what is required against what you are actually doing; Capricorn: you will have a purposeful approach and will make the most progress once you realise how useful this technique is and what it can do for you.

If you are an Air Sign (Gemini, Libra and Aquarius), your basic approach is one of judging progress against intention (i.e. where you are against where you want to be). You are very interested in things of the mind. You are instinctively quite good at not getting carried away by impulse, and your actions are usually guided by thought and reason, so you too are slower at getting caught in the web in the first place. However, you do tend to intellectualise your feelings, and your thoughts are generally organised and communicated rather than applied in practice, so you will probably find it easy to talk 'the talk' but find it difficult to actually start doing it. Like the Fire Signs, you need to acknowledge the situations where you could have been a fly on the wall – think, 'I should be a fly now', and aim to count to ten before you do or say anything – and then it will get easier for you. You will remain motivated by assessing things logically. You need to see your progress follows an obvious order. Gemini: you will be curious and inquisitive and will need to try many different methods; Libra: you will do best when you can balance one method against another one; Aquarius: you will need to assess how things were before you started the techniques contrasted with how things are now, and this will help you decide how to shape the future.

If you are a Water Sign (Cancer, Scorpio and Pisces), your basic approach is one of subjective experience. You generally take on the moods – including the cares and sorrows – of the people around you or of the places you visit, and so you can often be despondent or sad without knowing the reason. Therefore, you are going to have to try and create a lot more distance from your thoughts, actions and emotions than the other signs before you can become a disinterested observer. It is important for you to practise these techniques, though, because once you master them they will help you in your life as you won't get so caught up in emotions that are not your own. However, because your imaginative and emotional life is so deep and rich, once you embrace the technique you will do very well. Once you do decide to commit to the practice, you have great powers of tenacity and endurance and will carry on until you have mastered it. You will remain motivated by assessing your progress through your feelings - how you feel about what you are doing. Cancer: you will achieve the most when you experience a sense of belonging, so this initially needs to be linked where you first practise the technique; Scorpio: you will make the most progress when you can relate to the experiences of being a fly with intense feeling; Pisces: to make any progress you need to completely immerse yourself in the feelings so that you have the complete experience.

Tips to Help Bypass Your Ego

It will be hard initially to distance ourselves from our Ego, especially if we react to situations quickly like the Fire Signs or are emotional like the Water Signs. One way of starting is to try and label our emotion or feeling before we say or do anything. For example, if someone at work says you forgot to arrange a meeting, and you know that you didn't forget but your boss told you not to do it, then you are going to feel 'something' - defensive, angry, indignant - but before you leap in to start arguing with the person, consciously recognise your emotion. Step out of your Ego (be a fly!) and examine how you feel; then you can tell yourself, 'I feel annoyed that she thought I didn't arrange the meeting'. Then you will be more able to speak rationally and calmly and resolve the situation without resorting to frayed tempers or stress levels rising. Even counting to ten before you speak will help; it will give that bit of distance from your emotion, enabling you to detach from your Ego slightly. And the more you practise this, the better at it you will become.

Being a fly on the wall is linked to our ability to go through life on autopilot. Autopilot is basically the opposite of mindfulness; it is when our mind is disengaged from the present and stuck in habits we formed long ago. Autopilot is useful in that it allows us to carry out the basic functions of life (dressing, eating, walking etc.) without them taking up all of our attention. It is what we use once we have learnt a new skill - for example, driving a car, or touch typing; eventually the new skill becomes automatic and we can do it without thinking about it: we do it on automatic pilot. This can sometimes be desirable, as your mind can focus on something else that requires conscious attention, but it can work against us, particularly in the way we process our emotional lives. Ideally, with each emotional experience we encounter, we should reflect on how we felt about past experiences that were similar and remember what we did and how we responded. If we did not have a desirable or happy outcome last time, we should use our reflections to try to attain happier outcomes in the future by changing our emotional response to the situation. Problems occur when we repeat our emotional responses automatically (on automatic pilot), offering the same emotional reactions to similar situations, even though the outcome previously was not ideal. This is why it is easy for other people to 'push our buttons' – we automatically respond to triggers in the same way each time.

Like experiencing flow, being a fly on the wall is a great way to start experiencing mindfulness and beginning to reap the benefits of it. We should aim to distance ourselves from our automatic thoughts, actions and emotions as often as we can – even if we only manage it for a second, it is the first step towards being mindful. The more we can control our thoughts, actions and emotions then the more mindful we will be, and the more of its benefits we will gain.

> *Many of us are living on autopilot.*
> *We eat, but we do not taste.*
> *We hear, but we do not listen.*
> *We see, but we do not look.*
> *We touch, but we do not feel.*
> *This is why mindfulness matters.*
> *It helps us to live a more conscious life.*
> *~ Lauren Fogelmersy*

3. Attention and Sensation

Mindfulness involves observing what's going on without judging it. We direct our attention inwards and observe what we are thinking and feeling, but we also notice what sensations we are experiencing. In mindfulness practice, we choose where to put our focus. Things will always happen – a phone will ring, a clock will tick – but we decide not to engage with these sensations and instead redirect our attention to our chosen focus. We can focus on any of our senses. We can be aware of what we can hear, or what we can see, or what we can feel with our fingertips, or on our skin, or with other nerves. Or we can be aware of our bodily sensations like breathing or muscle tension.

Remember we need to be non-judgemental and compassionate when we practise mindfulness, and remember that things are unlikely to go smoothly, at least initially. For example, while you are trying to be mindful, you may suddenly become aware that you have a song playing in the back of your head, and that you've been trying to remember the name of it. You are immediately going to put yourself back to being a fly on the wall in this moment, and then again after the next stray thought, and the next one, and so on. If you find that you (or, more accurately, your Ego) have judged yourself negatively for not being able to stick to your goal of being a fly on the wall, that's fine too. Try not to judge the fact that you have judged yourself. It's the same thing for positive judgments. If you find that you were able to be a fly on the wall for seven seconds and realised that you have just congratulated yourself, you must try to move on from that.

Mindfulness is achieved by bringing ourselves into the present moment, identifying with our senses and putting our consciousness into a specific area of our body or into a sensation. This type of focus can be done almost anywhere at any time, in many different ways and for any length of time you like. That makes it ideal for signs like Aries, Sagittarius or Gemini, who get bored very quickly, as there is always a different thing they can do and there are no rules. I may sometimes use the word 'exercises' when talking about particular practices, but of course, exercise is not quite the right word, as it implies effort and technique. The only effort we need to apply is the decision to start, and then to continue until we stop. We cannot do anything wrong, there is no particular 'right' way - that's just us making a judgement about ourselves.

You need to find a way to deal with the thoughts that will inevitably come to the forefront of your mind when you try to be mindful. You may be able to deal with them by being a fly on the wall, but some people find this quite hard to do, especially Earth signs. You need to find a technique that enables you to recognise that the Ego has had a thought, then be able to release that thought calmly, without judgement or comment. You could visualise your thoughts as a river – your thoughts are streaming along in front of you, and every now and then the Ego pushes one out of the river into your conscious mind. This is a good analogy for Water signs. You are going to think 'My Ego has sent a thought,' and you are going to release it back into the river, so that it drifts away. Or you could imagine your thoughts as clouds, brushing past you; this is good for Air signs. Sometimes the Ego pushes a thought into your head; just put the thought in a balloon and release it to float way into the sky. Or you could imagine your thoughts from the Ego as leaves, falling from a tree and landing on the ground. You are going to calmly brush the thoughts away; this is good for Earth signs. Finally, you can imagine your Ego thoughts just popping into existence, lit up in front of you. You are going to acknowledge them, then move your attention away, letting them 'turn off' and vanish; this is a good technique for Fire signs.

Thoughts are always going to come into our head and distract us from your chosen focus. These thoughts often bring emotions, too: we may feel guilty or angry: we may think, 'I don't want to be thinking this, it's disturbing my mindfulness practice' - in this case we have just made a judgement. In mindfulness, we aim not to judge intruding thoughts and emotions, so we need to register our awareness of them, and notice how they make us feel, then focus our attention back on our breathing (or whatever we are doing), releasing our thoughts in whatever way we find best.

What will happen is that, with practise, we will eventually be able to achieve the ability to bring our attention back to focusing on the present moment. We should always start each mindfulness practise with three aims: firstly, each session is new, so don't have any expectations (which includes not comparing this session with any previous ones); secondly, we should aim to try and do our best to keep our attention on our chosen sensation, and it should be the only goal we have; and, finally, if we deviate from this goal, use a combination of self-compassion and non-judgment to correct ourselves.

Once the mindfulness session is over and to motivate ourselves for the next time, we should remember that there is no such thing as a bad mindfulness session. This is just not wishful thinking. Several studies have shown that what's most important in mindfulness practice is consistency. As long as we have sincerely tried to focus our attention, we will have a taken at least a small step towards becoming better at being mindful in any situation. So, basically, if we have patience and keep practising mindfulness, we will see the results. This means we need to make mindfulness such a priority that we work out a way to practice it at least a couple of minutes each day, no matter what. And, once we make that a non-negotiable goal, everything else will follow.

For all of these Attention and Sensation exercises,

the astrology signs need to use the same principles as for the breathing exercises. However, the impulsive, quick-to-get-bored signs (you know who you are!) should aim to start with shorter sessions and work up. These relaxation exercises are beneficial for every sign, but Aries, Gemini and Sagittarius will need a bit more effort to achieve the benefits. Signs that enjoy sensory experiences such as Taurus, Cancer, Leo, Pisces, Libra and Scorpio should be able to progress quickly once they start practising this type of mindfulness regularly. Capricorn and Virgo may struggle with this initially (as Virgo may feel inhibited and worried, unsure of what to do, and Capricorn won't see the point of it to begin with, but both Signs need to persevere if possible.). Scorpio should take to this easily and become very passionate about what they do. Aquarius will just want to do something very different and original! Focusing on sensation as a type of mindfulness is difficult at first, but it gets easier very quickly once we commit to practising it regularly. Just remember, we are only aiming for five minutes a day, at least to start with (and not even all in one go!). Even an Aries can achieve this!

Breathing

When first practising mindfulness, most people find it easier to observe a bodily sensation and, from research, it seems that observing the breath is one of the easiest things to do. There are many reasons why breath is a good thing to observe. It is constantly changing; we're always breathing in or breathing out, or holding our breath, so it's a little more interesting to observe than, say, the sensations on our hands. However, one of the first things we learn through mindfulness is that nothing is intrinsically boring. Indeed, boredom is simply a lack of attention; pay sufficient attention and the mere experience of breathing can keep us occupied for months. Breathing is easier to focus on than our thoughts, or other sensations - it's more obvious than our heartbeat, for example. Breathing is also something that is right on the edge of being voluntary (under our control) and involuntary (out of our control), which allows us to practice the idea of 'letting go' of control.

The first step in using breathing as a focus for attention is just to become aware of our breathing in the first place.

Breathe normally for a minute, then make your 'out' breath longer than your 'in' breath. This is automatically calming. Breathing in is what we do before we take action, getting ready to create energy and 'do' something, while breathing out is what we do after we have done something and are releasing stress. You don't have to count while you breathe or hold your breath, just exhale for longer than you inhale.

This is something we can do at any time; we don't need to do it in a specific mindfulness session. Do it when stuck in traffic, or in a boring meeting, or waiting in a queue. It will immediately calm our mind and focus our thoughts and emotions, and although our mind will mostly be concentrating on this, we should remember to release any random thoughts the Ego sends our way.

There are numerous other ways of engaging with breathing as a form of mindfulness. As well as the 'shorter inhale, longer exhale', we can count while we breathe.

A simple version of this is:
* count to four while you inhale
* hold your breath for a count of four
* count to four while you exhale
* hold your breath again for another count of four

Counting enables us to focus our mind and release random Ego thoughts. You may not want to count to four which is fine - you can count any number you like! You can inhale and exhale to one count and hold your breath to another count (e.g. inhale and exhale for a count of five, hold your breath for a count of three), or to a different number for each (e.g. inhale for four, hold your breath for two, exhale for three, hold your breath for five. Although, to be honest, that sounds like a very Aquarian way of approaching it!). You can vary it as much as you like; there are no rules for this, and it doesn't matter what you do as long as you keep your attention on your breathing. You can also do it for as long as you like, which is good for signs that get bored quickly and don't always finish what they start. Everyone can achieve with this!

A similar technique involves counting when we inhale, exhale and hold our breath, but this time we visualise a four-sided shape as we breathe.

For example, if you want to visualise a square:

* count to four as you inhale, while mentally tracing up the side of the square

* hold your breath for four as you mentally trace along the top

* exhale for four as you mentally trace down the other side

* hold your breath for four as you mentally trace along the bottom

If you find it difficult to visualise, you can follow the shape (lines) of a window or a mirror or a picture - use something with four sides that you can mentally trace around. It will work in a similar way to mentally visualising, and you may even find that starting with this technique leads you to being able to visualise a shape yourself later on.

Another way of breathing involves visualising light moving as you breathe:

* as you inhale, imagine white light entering your body

* hold your breath and 'see' this light flow down

through your body, filling you with peace and absorbing all of your negative energy

* exhale and 'see' the negative energy leaving your body

This is particularly good for the Water signs as they can release any emotional stress or tension in a practical way, but all signs benefit from this.

You can also recite something as you breathe, either under your breath or in your mind. Something simple like an affirmation or a short prayer, or even a nursery rhyme would do, unless you love a specific piece of poetry or know some novels off by heart! This is particularly good for the Air signs, as they enjoy talking. Think (or say out loud) the first line as you breathe in, and then think (or say out loud) the second line as you breathe out, and so on.

For example:

* inhale while (mentally) reciting *Humpty Dumpty sat on a wall*

* exhale while (mentally) reciting *Humpty Dumpty had a great fall*

* inhale while (mentally) reciting *All the King's horses and all the King's men*

* exhale while (mentally) reciting *Couldn't put Humpty together again*

You can also 'sing' in your head if you prefer. As long as you link the words to your breathing you will be practising mindfulness.

How we approach these different breathing exercises will depend upon our sign. Some signs like having structure and rules and will need to know exactly what they are doing. Taurus, Cancer, Virgo, Libra and Capricorn will need to plan in advance exactly which technique they are going to use and be very clear on what they are going to do. Pisces, Aquarius, Scorpio and Leo will need to know the steps involved and in what way they aim to go with it. Aries, Gemini and Sagittarius will just want to read everything through once and then make a start, with no planning at all.

Relaxation

Paying attention to bodily sensations is harder than focusing on breathing, but relaxation – or being aware of the state of our muscle tension – is probably the easiest thing to start with. We can do this on its own or link it with breathing. Put your conscious attention into an area of your body – it is best to start either at the feet and work up the body, or at the head and work down – and relax the muscles there. If you are not sure what that feels like, tense that area first so that you can feel the difference.

Imagine you are relaxing from your feet up. Clench your toes then relax them. Feel the muscles loosen and spread out, and experience a sense of lightness and calm in your toes. Then proceed to do this with all areas of your body, continuing with the feet, calves, shins, back of thighs, front of thighs etc. You will not be able to tense every area of your body before relaxing it, but you can 'feel' your muscles spreading out and softening in those areas. To relax your face and head, ensure you have relaxed your shoulders first (we always carry so much tension in our shoulders!), then relax your tongue away from the roof of your mouth, relax your jaw ,then your cheeks and forehead and, to relax your scalp, imagine you have just taken off a tight hat or headband. You should be able to feel the muscles in your scalp soften and release their tension.

Whole-body relaxation is nice when we are lying in bed before falling asleep, or if we are ending an exercise session, but we can relax specific areas if that is more appropriate to our situation. For example, you can relax your head and shoulders if you are short on time or are stuck in a traffic jam. There are no rules to any of this, so just do what feels right or do whatever you think you can manage. Remember, the aim is to achieve what we set out to do, so set realistic targets.

An example of a whole-body relaxation:
    * do this exercise lying on the floor or on a bed, or sitting in a chair
    * inhale deeply and point your toes; hold your breath for a count of four, then exhale, releasing any tension and letting your feet relax and open
    * inhale deeply and flex your feet up, tensing

your calf muscles; hold your breath for a count of four, then exhale, releasing any tension and letting your legs and feet relax

* inhale deeply and clench the muscles on your upper thigh, above the kneecaps; hold your breath for a count of four, then exhale, releasing any tension and letting your thighs relax and roll open

* inhale deeply and clench your buttocks and lower abdomen; hold your breath for a count of four, then exhale, releasing any tension and letting your muscles relax

* inhale deeply and take the breath into your abdomen, letting it extend out; hold your breath for a count of four, then exhale, releasing any tension and letting your muscles relax

* bend your elbows and clench your fists, inhaling deeply and tightening the muscles in your arms; hold your breath for a count of four, then exhale, releasing any tension and letting your muscles relax, opening your hands and letting your fingers gently curl

* inhale deeply and raise your shoulders up to your ears; hold your breath for a count of four, then exhale, releasing any tension and letting your muscles relax

* inhale deeply and bring your hands in front of your chest, pressing your palms together; hold your breath for a count of four, then exhale, releasing any tension and bringing your arms down and letting your muscles relax

* inhale deeply and expand your lungs and

chest; hold your breath for a count of four, then exhale, releasing any tension and letting your muscles relax

* inhale deeply and lift up your head; hold your breath for a count of four, then exhale, releasing any tension and letting your muscles relax. If you are in a chair, roll your head from side to side as you inhale and exhale

* inhale deeply and raise your shoulders up to your ear; hold your breath for a count of four, then exhale, releasing any tension and letting your muscles relax

* inhale deeply and frown, tensing your forehead; hold your breath for a count of four, then exhale, releasing any tension and letting your muscles relax

* inhale deeply and relax your scalp (imagine you have just taken off a tight hat or headband); hold your breath for a count of four, then exhale, releasing any tension and letting your muscles relax

* inhale deeply and open your mouth wide; hold your breath for a count of four, then exhale, releasing any tension and slowly close your jaw, letting your muscles relax

* inhale deeply and press your tongue against the roof of your mouth; hold your breath for a count of four, then exhale, releasing any tension and letting your tongue relax

* inhale deeply and hold your breath for a count of four, then exhale, releasing any tension and let-

ting your whole body relax

*continue breathing until you are ready to end the session

We can relax and be mindful in other ways too - for example, having a massage or treatment, as at that time we are (hopefully!) focusing on the moment. We should try to feel the way our muscles respond to the movements of the therapist and try to 'sink' into the bed or chair while it is going on.

Conscious Sensation

This is when we become aware of the sensations that we feel on (or in) our body by focusing our conscious mind into specific areas in our body. If you decide to observe your breath as a mindfulness practice, you will simply become aware of the sensations that you feel on a particular part of your body as you breathe. For example, you could focus on the sensations on the walls of your nostrils as you breathe in and breathe out. As you do this you may notice that both breathing in and breathing out puts some pressure on the walls of your nostrils. Or you may start to notice that the incoming breath is just a little bit cooler than the outgoing one. Or that the breathing happens mainly through one nostril, either the left or the right, for a period of time, before it switches to the other nostril. If you continue to pay attention to the sensations that breathing causes in and around your nostrils, you may start to notice even more subtle things like the follicles inside your nasal passage moving with your inhalations and exhalations. Or that your inhalations cool not just your nasal passage, but the inside of your mouth, your palate. In the process of becoming aware of all this, your breath is likely to become calmer, and quieter, subtler and slower. Of course, noticing all this is only possible if we aren't distracted by our thoughts. This is where our ability to merely observe our thoughts, and let them pass by, as if we were flies on the wall, comes in. Being a fly on the wall, it's best not to judge ourselves for negative thoughts such as 'I can't even focus on my breath for five seconds at a time!' Just forget what happened in the past and come back to becoming aware of the sensations caused by the act of breathing.

Breathing will also bring other sensations to our body. We will feel our chest and abdomen rise and fall, or we may be aware that our heartbeat slows. It is quite hard not to use breathing as the tool to access bodily sensations, but focusing on both at the same time is still being mindful.

We can also become aware of other feelings in our body. If you are sitting in a chair, you can feel the pressure from the floor on your feet and the pressure from the chair on the backs of your legs. Feel your feet relaxing into the ground and your legs sinking into the chair. If you're lying on the floor or in bed, feel the surface beneath you on your body, then relax into it. Combined with breathing, this is one of the easiest mindful practises to do.

Using Our Senses

This is when we focus our conscious mind on our practical senses; realistically, this usually means using our hearing, our vision and our sense of touch. Again, this can be combined with breathing. There are many levels of mindfulness associated with practical sensations. It can be a quick ten second practice, just to calm us down if we are getting stressed or to focus our mind if we feel it wandering, or it can be a complete hour-long meditation. Do whatever you feel is needed at that particular moment.

For example, if you are waiting for something or someone and you can feel yourself getting impatient or stressed, identify five sounds that you can hear and then work out which one is furthest away. Or count how many different shades of green you can see. Or calculate how many petals are on the flowers in the vase. Take some deep breaths. Can you smell anything? These quick exercises bring your thoughts, emotions and actions back under your control.

Using our senses can be linked to other mindful practices. For example, when walking, how many different sounds can you hear? You can listen to the sound your feet make on the path or listen for how many different bird songs you can hear. You can also use the nerves in your skin. Can you feel the breeze on your skin, or the heat of the sun? Can you discern the weather with your eyes closed?

Spending time in nature is a very powerful way of achieving mindfulness. There are so many different ways of relating to our body and the sensations it experiences:

* You can be near water which will give you a very specific set of experiences – what you can see, what you can hear, and water has a very high energy which can recharge most people, especially Water signs.

* You can be in a wood or forest, or just near a tree – trees have a powerful energy and can help boost our own energy, especially Earth signs

* You can be in a garden amongst flowers – colours are a form of therapy and can change your mood. Really look at the shape and colour of the petals, and be aware of the scents the flowers produce. Touch the leaves of the plants. How do they feel? Are they smooth or hairy or spiky? Soft or rough? Run your hands down the stems. Are they slender and fragile. Tough or woody? Fire and Air signs in particular benefit from the variety of experiences available in a garden.

* You can be on a beach – the sea gives off lots of negative ions which helps your energy, and the

sand (or pebbles) can give you different sensory experiences. What does it feel like? What does it sound like? Is it warm to the touch, or cool? Is it wet or dry? All signs can increase their energy and find it easier to be mindful near the sea.

Wherever we are, in whatever setting, there are so many ways that we can engage our senses. Start right this minute and make it a daily habit.

Mindfulness and Animals

There are many ways we can practise mindfulness around animals. To a degree, all of this can also apply to our interactions with our children, but it is harder to do with children as we can use language with them. Using language takes us a level away from bare awareness, and we tend to be too subjectively invested in our children to be able to create the mental distance necessary to achieve mindfulness.

Dogs, in particular, can help us become aware of the principles of mindfulness. Dogs live completely in the moment – think how happy they are when we return home, or when it's dinner time, or play time. Dogs also bring us a very good way to help us practise stepping outside our Ego, as there are always going to be times when our dog doesn't behave the way we want him to. He might bark at the dog over the road or run around crazily when a visitor comes to the house, or he might refuse to go into the vets. Too often we forget that we are in a partnership with our dog and we are an important link in our dog's behaviours. Dogs react to our energy and body signals more than we are consciously aware of; our dogs tend to respond to our energy and body language rather than our words. Knowing this will help us when we are dealing with our dog's perceived problem behaviours. (Remember these are only a problem to us - to our dog, his behaviour makes perfect sense.) It is really important that we take the time to step back from our dog's unwanted behaviour; be a fly on the wall - non-judgementally and objectively assess what you feel (probably embarrassment and guilt) and let it go without getting caught on the web which will trigger further thoughts, emotions or actions.

How to Encourage Mindfulness in Your Dog

We all get into the habit of walking our dogs the same way, in the same few places. We walk at a certain speed, go in a specific direction, and move the dog along when he wants to stop and sniff. We throw balls and frisbees for our dogs and take them jogging with us, but these things do not lower stress (ours or the dog's!) or use the dog's senses in a meaningful way.

Obviously, we always have lots of things to do in our busy lives and can't necessarily spend ages walking the dog in a mindful way, but we should aim to do a 'dog-centred' mindful walk two or three times a week to see the difference it makes to both us and our dog.

* Use a harness (don't have the lead on the collar, which is uncomfortable for dogs). Use a long line if necessary (not an extendable lead). The walk needs to be relaxed with a loose lead. Let the lead be quite long – the dog is not to be 'glued' to your side; he needs the freedom to wander and sniff. Ideally, the dog should be off-lead (if this is appropriate) where he can walk at his own pace and direction. Remember, our dogs take cues from us, so if we are hurrying along, our dog will not stop to wander. We need to slow down too!

* Go to different places regularly. Our dog needs variety in what he gets to experience and the opportunity to explore new and interesting (for him) environments. A walk along a town street may not seem like much fun, but, as long as our dog is comfortable in this environment, there are so many new smells and experiences for him to process. We should never take our dog to places he cannot cope with (watch his body language). Walks should be pleasurable for our dog; as such, if necessary, we should keep to places we know our dog enjoys while he builds his confidence. We should also avoid other dogs and people if we know our dog is not confident around them – we can use other days to work on desensitising him to these triggers.

* Walk slowly! It is important to allow the dog to make choices – for example, to walk on our left or right, in front of or behind us, decide where to go, at what speed, where to stop etc.

* Occasionally, sit somewhere and watch the word go by. There is no hurry, no pressure…

These types of walks will increase the bond between us and our dog, and we will find they benefit us, too, as we will be more mindful, calmer and less stressed.

Other animals can also help us practise mindfulness – cats, horses, rabbits, parrots, or any pet you live with. Using our sense of touch is very beneficial if we live with (or can be around) an animal that we can handle. However, we should only do this if the animal is completely comfortable with us being next to them and touching them. The animal must have complete choice and be able to move away at any time. Never restrain any animal. We can sit or lie with our cat, dog, rabbit, horse (or whichever animal we have) and gently rest a hand on their body, taking slow, deep breaths and noticing how our pet is breathing. Are they breathing slower or faster than us? If we change our rate of breathing, does theirs change too? We can feel their fur with total mindfulness, using our sense of touch. Is it soft or coarse, fine or thick? Does it feel warm or cool? We can slowly move our hand over their body. Are any areas different, are there hot spots or cooler spots?

Is the fur softer in places? Are there any areas that they don't want us to touch – do they move away? Doing mindfulness practise with our pets is a really good way to increase the bond between us and them and it helps us to learn more about our pet, lowers the blood pressures of both us and our pet, and increases our mindfulness abilities. If our pet doesn't have fur (a reptile or a bird, for example), we can do the same mindfulness practice, but instead we can feel the texture of the skin, or the softness of the feathers - whatever is appropriate for our pet.

Meditation

Meditation is the name we give to the process of becoming aware (or mindful) in order to achieve a mentally clear and emotionally calm state. All of the different ways of practising mindfulness are forms of meditation. (The words 'meditation' and 'mindfulness' are often used interchangeably). There is no right or wrong way of doing it, and there are no real rules - we need to find a way that suits us and just keep doing that. There are some common myths about meditation which tend to put some people off – they may think that we need to wear special clothes, that we need to sit cross-legged on the floor, that we need to set aside 'formal' structured time, or that we need to be spiritual etc. Meditation (or mindfulness) just means being in the present moment without judgement.

If our Ego tries to interfere, we must try to ignore it.

There are many pre-recorded meditation CDs we can buy, or we can listen to mediations on the internet. These typically consist of relaxing music, with someone speaking over it, giving guidelines for us to follow. They usually start with breathing exercises, followed by directed visualising, for example: 'You are walking on a path through a forest'; or, 'You see a key on the floor'; or, 'You are walking barefoot through the warm sand'; or, 'You are surrounded by white light'. Obviously, everyone will visualise something different and that's fine. Meditation like this is a way for us to lose our Ego for a while and allow our subconscious mind to have time in our awareness.

We can do a meditation by ourselves if we prefer, without using a CD or something from the internet. We can learn a technique off by heart, or we could record ourselves saying it and then follow our own instructions. We could even make one up for ourselves or use one from a book or a website.

This is an example mediation to connect us to our higher self or inner child:
   (reproduced with kind permission from Donna Maxine)

If you are on strong medication or suffer from epilepsy, always consult your doctor before meditating.

* Make sure you are sitting or lying comfortably in a place where you won't be disturbed.

* Close your eyes and count backwards, 10 down to 1, and take a deep breath and exhale. Repeat this a couple of times.

* Then visualise yourself sitting either in a clearing in a wood, or at a picnic table, or in a chair in a beautiful park, or another favourite place where you feel safe and comfortable. 'See' yourself surrounded by trees where the grass is very green and soft under your feet. Imagine you can feel the warm sun, and you may see birds flying overhead. You may even smell the grass or nearby flowers, and you can feel yourself becoming more and more relaxed.

* Take a deep breath and exhale, and this time when you breathe in, visualise the breath as white shimmering light. Feel that light filling every cell in your body with beautiful, shimmering, white, healing, liquid light. You can see your cells as bubbles, becoming lighter.

* Allow yourself to become calm, your breath slowing and your shoulders relaxing. Feel this happening all over your body, down your arms, elbows, fingers, spine, hips, thighs, calves, ankles and feet. Feel yourself gently easing your back against the comfortable chair and being at one with your surroundings.

*Picture the sunlight shining on you and warming your body, feel the warmth on your face, notice the dappled rays of sunlight filtering through the trees into the clearing where you are sitting.

*You know you are safe and totally peaceful and very, very relaxed.

* You become aware of somebody walking into the clearing. You see a person who looks just like you, but they are made of gorgeous, glittery light. This is your higher self. This is the aspect of you that knows everything you are supposed to go through in this lifetime and everything you have been through in any previous lives. Your higher self is there to guide your soul on your life path – you may want to have a conversation and ask any questions that you need answers to. Don't worry if the answer to your questions do not come to you straight away; you may find they will pop into your mind while you are sleeping later tonight. It may take several attempts to practise this meditation correctly if you are new to this.

* After you have finished speaking with your higher self, give them a hug and know that you can connect any time you need help or guidance to deal with any problems you are struggling with.

* As you hug them, imagine feeling a beautiful, swirling light pouring down from the sky, surrounding you both. Your aura is like a glittery globe of light particles mixed with glitter ... as it settles, there is a mixing of your own energy and the energy of your higher self, combined. This will

help you link with your intuition.

* As you go to leave this clearing in the trees, you see a beautiful velvet cloak hanging on one of the branches of the trees, and you know it's your cloak of protection. Place it around your shoulders to protect your energy field.

* Now visualise seven rings of light surrounding your body, around your feet, your hips, your tummy, your chest and your throat, moving up to your forehead, and finally just above the top of your head.

* Count from 1 to 10 and take a final deep breath, wiggle your fingers and toes, gently stamp your feet and open your eyes.

Remember that although most people think of 'meditation' as the practise of visualising something, any of the Attention and Sensation techniques are a form of meditation.

Mandalas and Labyrinths

Mandalas and labyrinths are a good meditation tool and can also help us to develop our mindfulness skills, as we may find that we need to be quite disciplined to keep focused. They are good for 'fly on the wall' practice and also beneficial when we are doing any mindful breathing.

Mandalas are sometimes called 'magic circles' and have been used for thousands of years in many different religions, especially Buddhism and Hinduism, to help with meditation and healing. They can help us to stay grounded, calm and balanced. There are many designs for mandalas, and no rules, although they are generally symmetrical – although they don't have to be. Dream catchers are mandalas, as are rings in a tree stump, and also cobwebs!

We can draw our own mandala and then colour it in if we wish (this is also good for creativity, and remember, we should try to use our non-dominant hand), or we can colour a pre-drawn one.

Creating Our Own Mandalas

The actual drawing of a Mandala is a meditation in itself (think about doodling while on the phone), so we can use this same technique and let our pen or pencil move without thinking too deeply about what to do next.

There are two ways of proceeding: we can have a piece of paper with a circle already drawn on it (use a plate or something to draw round to get the circle); or we can use lines to split our page into sections, like we are cutting a cake, and add the edges later. With the pre-drawn circle, we can divide it into 4 and draw each section symmetrically with abstract designs, or we can have hearts or flowers – anything we like. For the other way (using lines), we can imagine we are dividing a cake and draw several intersecting lines to give us either 4 or 8 sections, and add the edges later.

Draw in whatever designs or symbols come to you; it can be symmetrical or not, whatever seems right for that particular design. You can draw each section with a different design – just do whatever you feel is right for you at that time. Each section could represent a different aspect of your life, or you could draw symbols for a particular area of your life (e.g. work, or love). It should all have significance for you and be personal to you, so let your intuition guide you as much as possible.

When you have finished designing and colouring your mandala, you can put it where you can see it, as the mindfulness you experienced while creating it will trigger a feeling of accomplishment and the subconscious need to repeat the experience.

Example of a mandala

Labyrinths, too, have been around for thousands of years, with labyrinth stone wall carvings, clay tablets and coins dating back to the Bronze Age. A Labyrinth is not a maze; a maze has blind dead ends that are used to confuse and trick the mind. A labyrinth is a spiral course having a single, winding, unobstructed path from the outside to the centre that is used to calm and relax. (The point of a maze is to find the centre; the point of a labyrinth is to find your centre). There are many large labyrinths in gardens or wellbeing retreats, and these are used for 'walking meditations'. As you walk, you can see all of the path, and, as it spirals inwards, you focus on where you are putting your feet (you can use any of the sensation techniques when doing this). When you reach the centre of the labyrinth, do some mindful breathing and assess how you are feeling, then retrace your path out of the labyrinth.

Labyrinths drawn on paper can be coloured in or used as a 'finger' labyrinth.

Creating Our Own Labyrinths

Creating a Labyrinth is different to a Mandala: we start with a cross, and add some lines in the corners, then add dots, and then join them up (see diagrams). We can make them as complicated or as simple as we like, and can colour it in if that is our choice (this is also good for creativity, and we should try to remember to use our non-dominant hand), or we can colour a pre-drawn one.

A drawn Labyrinth can also be used as a finger labyrinth.

Example of a labyrinth

How to do a 'finger' labyrinth meditation:

• Breathe with awareness until you are relaxed and then focus on the entrance to the labyrinth.

• Put the index finger of your non-writing hand on the paper, at the entrance to the labyrinth. (If you find this too awkward at first, use your writing hand. However, do keep trying your non-writing hand as this helps to keep your mind focused on the meditation due to the challenge it presents.)

• Slowly trace the pattern of the labyrinth with your finger, allowing your mind to let go of any thoughts and emotions, and focus solely on following the path of the labyrinth.

➢ When you reach the centre of the labyrinth, do some mindful breathing and assess how you are feeling, then retrace your path out of the labyrinth.

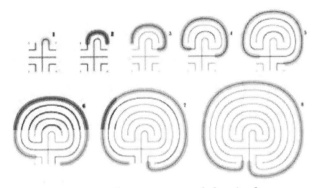

Drawing your own labyrinth

Astrology Signs and Their Approach to Attention and Sensation

• Aries

If you are Aries, you don't like to be told how to do things! You need the freedom of doing things your own way, so having control over what you do with regards to Attention and Sensation is very important. Because there are no rules to any of it, you can choose what to do and how long to do it for. Your thought processes are generally sharp, making you quick to grasp information. However, you must try to persevere with something and not give up when it gets a bit hard and just move on to something else. You have fresh, original ideas and a lot of enthusiasm for anything new and untried, but once the novelty has worn off, you are inter-ested in another new idea or project. (You never seem to have enough time to do all you want to!) For example, meditation CDs may be difficult for you as you will not always want to do what is said, or you will want to do it more quickly etc. But learning to follow guidelines set by others is an important lesson and will benefit you greatly once you master it. If you want to try meditation CDs, you need to choose a very short and simple meditation and build on this. Even with some of the other techniques (breathing, relaxing, using your senses), you should attempt to impose a bit of structure rather than just leaping around from one to the other. You tend to follow your impulses rather than your good sense, but at least being able to choose how, what, where and for how long will give you the control you feel you need in order to actually get started. Others cannot suggest what you should do; because you can be headstrong and irrational, you want to feel that what you do is your own choice. You may suffer from headaches, which may be the effect of suppressed anger, so it is really important that you manage to find a technique that works for you and allows you to release your inner frustrations. It is hard for you to sit still – you always have to be busy, especially with your hands. Therefore, working on attention and sensation techniques is very important for you, as you need to learn how to quiet your ever-active mind.

• Taurus

If you are Taurus, you need to know what you are doing, so you will benefit from a structured routine. Using a CD or following a prescribed method will help you to keep going, but you need to start with short sessions. You have a psychological need to finish what you start, but you also get bored quite quickly, so something you can complete within a shorter timeframe would be good initially. You can build up to longer sessions once you feel you have mastered the techniques. You don't like to feel rushed or pressured, so something that allows you to work at your own pace is important, and you need to be clear on what you want to do before you begin, as you don't like changing things once you have started. You need to be pushed into change sometimes, as learning to be more adaptable is an important lesson for you, so you could try a new technique or alter something within your normal routine eventually. You need to see the point of the things you do, so you should understand the benefits of the activities before you start – this will keep you more motivated. You will do very well at anything you set your mind to because you have the ability to concentrate and follow a project through to its completion. You will need to do something that brings benefits to you quite quickly, as you like to do things that you know are useful. You think with your feelings quite a lot, and you will reject a logically correct statement if it doesn't fit in with your feelings. Common sense and experience is very important to you when it comes to making decisions and assimilating information; therefore, the more you can practise the techniques, the easier you will find them and the more motivated you will be to continue. You will do very well at the relaxation techniques, as massages and treatments suit you.

• Gemini

If you are Gemini, you always need to feel that you have a choice, and you love variety, so being able to dip in and out of different techniques will help to keep you motivated. You like to try a little bit of everything, but concentration and disciplined study are not your strong points. Due to your love of being involved in several things at once, you will benefit from the different attention and sensation techniques, but you do need to learn to focus and not just skim the surface of everything. You love being involved in multiple things at once and are quick to grasp new concepts, but equally quick to lose interest in an idea or project once your curiosity has been satisfied. The fact you can't concentrate on anything for long periods of time can be a problem as you won't try anything long enough for it to become familiar, nor will you discover the benefits. Make this an area of focus and build up your attention. You find it hard to finish what you start, so you should aim for short sessions to begin with so you can actually achieve them. Short sessions (and short meditations etc.) will also stop you from getting bored. You should try all of the different methods, ideally by following a list, as this will help you to impose some structure. You need to learn to develop control of your thoughts and actions in order to be successful at mindfulness. You need to find your focus, stay with it, and develop perseverance. You will need to persist with these techniques as you can find it hard to control your mind, but you will benefit once you have mastered it - this is an important lesson for you. You have so much nervous energy that it can sometimes cause you stress, for which you must find an appropriate release. Once you can channel your mind, you will be able to balance your highly-strung nervous system, enabling you to experience the benefits of being mindful.

• Cancer

If you are Cancer, you are very connected to your memories, feelings and emotions, especially from the past. You like to hold on to the memories of things because it gives you security. You need to find Attention and Sensation techniques that evoke habits or memories from your past – at least initially. You are very interested in inner, subjective and personal issues, and your thinking is based more on feelings, intuition and personal experiences rather than reason or logic. Intellectual abilities and accomplishments, without feeling them heart or soul, mean little to you. You may have a problem in completely understanding a specific new technique; this is because you can so easily become emotionally involved with everything else that you tend focus on this instead of the technique itself. You would benefit from keeping a diary or notebook about your achievements in mindfulness, which will help to keep you motivated. You would also do better in small groups, as you will find it easier to focus with others present, and you will also be motivated by others. You need to learn to be more self-sufficient, though, so once you are comfortable with a particular technique in a group, you need to try it on your own. It is very important to you that you are in congenial surroundings, so doing things outside will benefit you, or you at least need to be in places that have positive vibrations. You can have difficulty in making decisions, so you will need 'pushing' into trying something different, or it could be that sometimes you may simply change your mind constantly. You should aim to develop your mental focus and control, as this is an important lesson for you. You are good at listening, so starting with using your sense of hearing may be beneficial. Your mind retains and absorbs knowledge easily, so once you have learnt something you will never forget it. You can be prone to worry, so you will need to be encouraged that you are doing fine! Once you feel comfortable with mindfulness, you will be able to swap and change between techniques easily.

● Leo

If you are Leo, you generally have strong opinions and love to express your thoughts energetically and dramatically. You wholeheartedly identify with your beliefs, so, if you can embrace mindfulness, you will do very well at it. You are usually very sure that your ideas are right, and you like to encourage others to think the way you do. You can contemplate new ideas and make them part of your own thinking, as long as no one is pressuring you to do so. You find it easier to embrace a new technique if you can think it was your idea! You will need to begin with a technique that allows you to show that you have achieved it, as it is important to you that others are able to recognise your abilities. Your own self-confidence will help you go far – indeed, your achievements can be considerable – but pride and self-importance could prove to be a problem, which is something you need to be aware of. An important lesson for you is to learn to do things quietly, behind the scenes. You have a distinctive style of self-expression, have many creative ideas, and you will want to have a voice in decision-making, especially if it concerns whatever you are planning to do. You tend to have ambitious thoughts and like a challenge, but you also need to accomplish what you set out to do, so starting with something that is achievable and not too difficult is the best way for you to get started. You have good intuition and can easily grasp the principles of what is required. Initially, you will need to be motivated by others; without someone to see how well you have achieved, you may not see the point of doing it, but, as you become more proficient in the practices, you will be able to do them for your own self-achievement. This is a valuable lesson for you.

• Virgo

If you are Virgo, you tend to be an exacting perfectionist with a clear, logical and analytical mind, and you have an aptitude for things that require meticulous attention to detail. You can, therefore, learn about subjects that require careful thinking and can also learn complicated techniques. The more intricate the techniques, the better you like them. You will need to study what is involved before starting, and ensure that you are very clear about what you are doing and why. You will benefit from techniques that have structure and definite steps and progression. Knowledge, ideas and theories don't really interest you unless they are useful in a practical, demonstrable way. You love to analyse, measure, and dissect everything, but in doing this you can miss nuances and subtle shades of feeling and meaning; this is an important lesson for you – you need to embrace your emotions more. You don't like the feeling of not being able to do something to the best of your ability, so will need to start with something achievable that you have spent time studying beforehand. You find it easy to articulate ideas in writing, so you could keep a diary that charts your progress and evaluates your techniques as you would find this motivational. You need to learn not to get too bogged down in details; you tend to over-think what you are doing. Mindfulness needs to be something you feel, not something you formulate. You have an interest in your health and wellbeing, so once you experience the benefits of mindfulness you will be very determined to continue with it; and, with your good powers of persuasion, you will motivate others to keep going too. It is very important for you to still your mind regularly as it is generally so busy, so you, in particular, would benefit from making mindfulness a regular thing.

• Libra

If you are Libra, you have an ability to see all sides of a subject and therefore find it hard to make a decision. You will need help from others to get started on learning a new technique, ideally one that pleases your fine aesthetic sensitivities. If someone else suggested a technique to you, though, you would not say you didn't like it as you often compromise to avoid hurting their feelings. However, you are usually actively seeking knowledge and mental stimulation; you have an agile, quick mind. You are very charming, which makes you good at subtly influencing others, so you will usually end up doing what you wanted. You like knowing everything that is involved in a subject before making up your mind. You love to compare things and find analogies. You tend not to be emotionally driven but will go by what you think is right. You need to be quite structured in your approach to mindfulness and learn not to depend on others' opinions – an important lesson is thinking for yourself. It is important that you are in a pleasant environment before starting a technique – being outside or in a specially designated room would be best, but as you learn to become more mindful, this will matter less. Recorded CDs etc. would be beneficial to you, as they usually contain beautiful music, which you love, and you are guided in what to do, which you also love. Once your confidence and experience in mindfulness grows, you will need to be encouraged to try many different techniques, as you sometimes like to stay with what you know and like rather than learn something new.

• Scorpio

If you are Scorpio, you have the ability to excel at practising mindfulness. You have excellent mental concentration and tend to become completely immersed in what you do. You often seem to know things at an instinctive, nonverbal level, and you prefer learning through direct experience or practise rather than via formal teaching. You have tremendous drive and determination to keep going and you take great pride in your achievements; once you set out to accomplish anything, you will work persistently towards your goal. Therefore, whatever you choose to do, you will achieve it and do it well. You like a challenge, so you will need something that stretches you slightly and just pushes you out of your comfort zone. You like to do things that demand continued, determined effort and intense concentration, so the more challenging the better. It is important that you find plenty of outlets for your highly powered emotional energy, so knowing how to do several techniques would be best. You will very quickly pick up the practices and learn how and what to do, but you will not reveal much of it to others; you like to keep your secrets. You are very intuitive and working with energies is beneficial for you, so you will do very well at the Attention and Sensation techniques. Learning how to control your emotions is an important lesson for you, so you would benefit from making mindfulness practice a regular part of your life (even more so than most of the other signs).

• Sagittarius

If you are Sagittarius, you have a quick, keen mind, but you don't particularly like details and may find it difficult to concentrate long enough to carry your ideas through to completion. You also need to feel free and uncommitted in your life and cannot bear to be tied down to people or situations – you can become rebellious and militant when frustrated. Therefore, you need the freedom to choose what to do, whenever you want to do it – this makes the Attention and Sensation exercises very beneficial for you. However, you are more concerned with theories, abstractions and concepts than with specific applications, so you must learn to concentrate enough to achieve success in the techniques. As you are so physical and enjoy outdoor activities, using your senses, or breathing while doing something outside, would be helpful to you while you learn to build up concentration. The challenge of a new subject is what interests you, so you tend to start new activities enthusiastically, then your energy tends to lessen as the project goes along and gets stuck in details, or the going gets a little rough, or it simply gets a little boring. You tend to study several similar things and have several projects going at the same time. You need to learn how to do many different techniques so that you can satisfy your need for variety. You want to gain experience, knowledge and wisdom, but you have to keep busy in order to attain this. You have a constant need for intellectual challenge; you never stop learning things and are unconcerned about the results – just 'doing something' is enough for you. However, an important lesson for you is to learn to do something fully, to the best of your ability. This will be easier for you if you really believe in what you are doing. However, you like the thought of something that encourages self-improvement.

● Capricorn

If you are Capricorn, you like to have a plan, so you will need to structure your approach to mindfulness. You tend to be methodical and formal, especially where decision-making is concerned. You are a practical thinker and do best when you are learning skills that will be useful in your life, so you will achieve great things once you have chosen what to do. You like to think and plan very carefully, and you don't want to jump to conclusions – you want to know the facts behind any statement or idea you hear. It would benefit you to research the techniques and benefits of mindfulness practices for yourself. You are then capable of working long hours with focused concentration and attention on whatever interests you. You will plan and patiently follow a realistic course which will lead to your eventual success. Serious-minded and studious, you enjoy (and profit from) quiet time alone, so you will gain a lot of benefit from mindfulness. An important lesson for you is to lighten up a bit and not take things so seriously, so you should try some of the more fun techniques, even though you may worry that they are not 'serious' enough. You are quite conventional, so would do best to start with the more common techniques initially - when you see results, your horizons may broaden. You will need encouraging to try different techniques once you have mastered a few, as you will want to continue improving the ones you already know, whereas it will be better for you to try alternatives. You have great determination in achieving the goals and purposes you set yourself and will not relax you have reached the target that you chose to aim for. You always do best if you have a goal in your sights, so you need to be structured with your practises so that you can see your progression.

• Aquarius

If you are Aquarius, you are a progressive and nontraditional thinker and are very open and receptive to new ideas. You will take to mindfulness very well, as long as you are allowed to approach it in your own time and do not feel forced into anything. You will want to follow your own principles regardless of what others think of you. You can be a bit impatient with others who are more traditionalist, or who you feel are unimaginative or are afraid to think about and try new things. You can have new and different ways of looking at things, so once a technique is mastered you are likely to alter it to suit yourself. You are capable and practical, but also can be prone to uncertain and sudden impulses, so you need flexibility in what you choose to do. You have the determination and persistence to achieve, and mindfulness will suit you very well, given its variable nature. You would do best to start with achievable aims, as sometimes your energy level is relatively low, which causes you to stop things before they are completed. You also need to feel that you have freedom in what to do, when, and for how long, so there is no feeling of being 'trapped'; you also hate dull routine. An important lesson for you is to use your heart as much as your head, so techniques which involve others in groups will help you with this. You are mentally independent, but you like to be with others in groups or societies based upon a common interest, so groups practising meditation (for example) would be good, as people are together but doing their own thing.

You get along well with others, but there are times when you need periods of quiet and solitude, so you will need to practise mindfulness alone too.

• Pisces

If you are Pisces, you can sometimes struggle to push yourself into doing anything that takes a lot of effort, but you can absorb knowledge in the most remarkable ways if you are interested in the subject area. You need to choose a technique that appeals to you – you will be emotionally drawn to what suits you. You need to keep grounded, so it would be best for you to do the practices in shorter sessions until you can control your thoughts and emotions. You need to learn how to be more practical and down-to-earth, as well as how to concentrate your energies on the present moment. You are sensitive to your environment and so should be careful of which locations you spend time in. Outdoors or being by water will benefit you. You struggle with too much structure or routine, so techniques that allow you to do what feels right at that time would be best, at least initially. You will enjoy doing what seems like fun and will like to feel that you are going with the flow and not being hemmed in by too much formality. However, leaning perseverance is an important lesson for you, so you need to develop your powers of concentration in baby steps. It is very important for you that you do learn how to be mindful – even more than most of the other signs – as you need time away from the chaos of the everyday world, to recharge your fluctuating energies. But, not too much time, as you tend to get too caught up with yourself and your problems. Mindfulness using visualisation techniques will be very effective for you, as your imagination is so powerful, but because of your tendency to get carried away, aim to keep things in perspective.

THE PARADOXES OF MINDFULNESS

Don't believe everything you think. Thoughts are just that – thoughts ~ Allan Lokos

The practice of mindfulness seems fraught with paradoxes! One paradox of mindfulness comes from the way that it is described with the fly on the wall analogy, which seems to be a little bit different from the way that mindfulness is often portrayed – i.e. being totally immersed in whatever is going on, rather than distancing yourself from it. Is this a paradox? How can we be both in touch with whatever's going on and still observe it from a distance? This is only a paradox if we think about mindfulness, rather than experience it or practise it. If we practise mindfulness, we will realise that the observing is not really going on from the perspective of the mind (or the Ego), but, rather, it is going on from the perspective of bare awareness or consciousness. This makes all the difference. When we observe through the Ego, there is a distance between ourselves and what we observe because the Ego tends to judge, categorise, comment, etc., which creates this distance. By contrast, when we observe from bare awareness, there is no distance between ourselves and the object of our observations.

Another apparent paradox of mindfulness is that, as it promotes response flexibility (the ability to choose how we respond to a stimulus rather than responding to it automatically), it must therefore reduce spontaneity. That is, it may seem that mindfulness would lead to a suppression of desires and instincts and lead us to make decisions based only on thoughtful deliberations. In reality, mindfulness doesn't lead to dependence on our thoughts, but, rather, it leads to independence. Mindfulness is ultimately about getting familiar with what's going on inside us, both at the level of the body and at the level of the mind. So, by practicing mindfulness, we'll get more intimately familiar with both what our sensations and feelings (i.e. your instincts) are telling us, as well as what our thoughts and deliberations (i.e. our rational side) are telling us. As a result, rather than reacting either too impulsively or too logically to a situation – both of which could lead to worse decisions – we're likely to respond in a manner that's more spontaneous and mature. However, this ability is something that will almost certainly take some time to acquire because, in the process of practicing mindfulness, it is likely that we will judge many of our instincts and feelings as wrong. This will not just inhibit our impulsivity, but also our spontaneity. However, over time, as we learn to recognise the difference between observing from our Ego and observing from bare awareness, and also learn how to steer ourselves into feeling present in the moment, we will see that mindfulness doesn't lower spontaneity but rather enhances it.

The third apparent paradox of mindfulness is that, even if we are mindful of something negative or unpleasant, we still feel good, or at least less bad, as a result. Most people are surprised that being mindful is a better way of feeling good than regulating their emotions or distracting themselves from these negative emotions. Accepting or embracing what we are feeling seems to be the last thing that we'd want to do if we are feeling bad. This is only a paradox if we confuse mindfulness with pondering about an event or analysing the negative experience as opposed to merely observing it. When we merely observe an unpleasant experience, we discover that it was more negative in our mind than it turned out to be as an experience. The saying, 'There's nothing to fear but fear itself,' captures this idea. Imagine you are travelling up a mountain by train and you see a big cloud that is very thick and covering the mountain top. It would seem that, if you were to enter the cloud, you wouldn't be able to see anything inside it. But once you do enter the cloud, it becomes insubstantial. In fact, once you're inside the cloud, it doesn't even seem like a cloud at all. The cloud may have completely hidden a whole village from a distance, but, once you enter it, you realise that you can see things quite clearly. Dealing with negative and unpleasant feelings are like these clouds. Once we've gathered up the courage to enter and explore these feelings, it turns out that we can handle them easily. Specifically, those feelings are reduced to sensations in various parts of our body. For example, the feeling that we all call anxiety reduces to the sensation of feeling hot and sweaty, among other things; the feeling that we call anger reduces to the sensation of tightness in our chest, among other things; and sadness reduces to the sensation of a pit in our stomach, etc. If we closely observe these sensations without judging them or getting caught up in thoughts, such as, "Why me? Poor me. Why do these things always happen to me?" we will notice that these sensations ebb, flow and mutate into other sensations, and ultimately vanish. Of course, not everyone is going to be capable of merely observing everything that's going on without getting caught up in musings and analyses, at least initially – these are skills that will come over time as our mindfulness experiences increase.

MAKING MINDFULNESS A HABIT

We are what we repeatedly do. Excellence, then, is not an act, but a habit ~ Aristotle

After reading this book, I hope that you are motivated to make mindfulness a new habit. It is very difficult for people to break old, established habits and make or acquire new ones. We touched on this when we talked about making a new road in our brain to rival our existing 'habit motorway'. Habits are formed when the motivational system of the brain works towards our goals, driving our behaviour and learning automatic responses and reactions: habits. When a habit forms, we associate a particular behaviour with the environment and our responses become automatic. The only thing that can stop us acting out our habitual behaviour (assuming we want to create new habits) is an area in our prefrontal cortex; it acts as a type of self-control mechanism. Unfortunately, this area of self-control is inefficient and can be impaired by stress, alcohol or drugs, and also by overuse. If we try and control our behaviour for too long, the self-control system doesn't work effectively; this is called the 'ego depletion effect'. Therefore, it makes sense to set things up so that we achieve success. Remember, the environment drives behaviour, so we should control our environment when we can so that it is harder for us to do the unwanted behaviour (or so that it is easier for us to do the required or desired behaviour). For example, if you want to lose weight but can't stop eating the ice cream that is in the freezer, don't buy it in the first place! And park further away from the shop door so that you have to walk more – be a bit more active. These simple changes to our environment will influence what we do or don't do. Therefore, when thinking of mindfulness, we should aim to start new behaviours in specific environments to encourage ourselves to create new habits.

When we first start mindfulness practice and aim to do our initial five minutes a day, we should start by doing the same things in the same places. For example, if you always walk your dog in the morning, then do some of the Attention and Sensation exercises every single time. Or, if you are always stuck in traffic every morning, do some of the quick relaxation techniques. Or aim to do some meditation for five minutes before lunch every day – it doesn't matter when you do it, as long as, for the first couple of weeks, it is consistent and predictable. What you will then find is that you automatically begin thinking about mindfulness when you are in that situation. This is the first step in incorporating mindfulness into our lives. We can then gradually increase how long we practise for, and then begin to do it in other places – we will eventually realise that we are practising mindfulness without even thinking about it.

Our ability to be mindful also depends on how stressed we feel. Even mild stress can cause a rapid and dramatic loss of prefrontal cognitive abilities. That is, by not being able to control our feelings, we lose our ability to make good decisions; also, the ego depletion effect will occur. Therefore, is important that we learn to manage and control our stress levels, and, although being mindful will eventually give us the ability to regulate our thoughts and feelings, at first, we need to be able to control our stress enough to actually start practising mindfulness in the first place.

HOW ASTROLOGY SIGNS DEAL WITH STRESS

*A child is born on that day and at that hour when
the celestial rays are in mathematical harmony
with his individual karma ~ Sri Yukteswar*

Understanding what it is about our temperament
that can lead to stress, and how we unconsciously
respond to it, will help us in our pursuit of mindfulness. We will be able to identify, and therefore
reduce, the things we instinctively do that eventually lead to stress and tension in our life. Being
aware of these factors is important both for how
we approach mindfulness and also how we can es-
tablish the best way for us personally to achieve
the very best from our mindful practices and our
life generally.

• Aries

If you are Aries, then you already know that you charge impulsively into things, impatient to get ahead. Your fast-paced, high pressure lifestyle can lead to general exhaustion and potential 'burn-out'. You can also put up with very adverse conditions if you think they will eventually get you what you want. The importance of learning how to manage your stress cannot be overstated. It is very common for you to have anger issues; your initial reaction to something that upsets you, or stops you getting your own way, is anger. You are the sign that can even hit the wall in frustration. Because you need constant action your stress can manifest in a physical way – you are the nail-biter, finger-drummer or foot-tapper of the zodiac. You are also prone to tension headaches that can sometimes be hard to get rid of. You are generally a self-sufficient sign, and if you are sad or in a bad mood you can easily restore your own energies. This is because you tend to be a very private person, and your first instinct will be to mask any anxiety you feel in order to maintain your reputation as powerful and in control. You may also attempt to counteract your stress with exercise, trying hard to reduce your inner turmoil with physical effort. This is the wrong approach for you, as the best way to soothe your soul is to keep your body and brain equally busy. Therefore, instead of mindlessly throwing yourself into intense cardio sessions or kickboxing classes, try something that stretches you physically but also calms your mind – yoga, for example. Your chosen method of relieving stress can still be physically demanding and engaging, but it also needs to encourage calm focus and self-assurance.

• Taurus

If you are Taurus, you always prefer to work slowly and methodically, as you do not perform well under pressure. You hate to feel hurried or rushed; this causes you to feel stressed and you can get quite stubborn in response. You tend to get quite anxious if things deviate from normal, but this does need to happen sometimes, as you need to learn to be more flexible and adaptable. You need to be allowed the time to think through and sort out your deeper feelings and motivations. You are also very influenced by your subconscious mind; if a seed gets planted in your mind, eventually it will grow enough for you to notice it and you then take it as a new idea to act upon. Find ways of planting these new ideas in order to motivate yourself. When you feel stressed, you have quite a few automatic strategies that you can use to deal with it, and you intuitively look for a distraction. However, instinctively, this will be something like curling up with a duvet and binge-watching something. You understand the concept that, after some time out, everything feels more manageable, so you may find yourself taking these 'mental health' days if you're feeling particularly overwhelmed. Try and have natural things around you – cotton, hessian, plants – as a sense of luxury is important to you and will help destress you. However, you need to push yourself out of your instinctive response to stress and do something active. Work on establishing a productive new routine that you can incorporate into your life, as this will help to energise you. Choose something that isn't going to bring any more pressure to your day, but that will make you feel in control and nurtured – learn to cook healthy meals, or get up a bit earlier so that you can have a relaxing breakfast, for example. Having regular massages, especially with essential oils, is very good at helping you manage your stress.

• Gemini

If you are Gemini, you know that you tend to stay one step ahead of everyone else because you live in your own mind. You mind is very quick and that, coupled with your endless thinking, often causes you to burn the candle at both ends, leading to nervous exhaustion. However, you generally don't like to have to deal with stress; you tend to internalise it, and push it down inside yourself, but this inner confusion inevitably takes its toll, and, depending on how emotionally connected you feel to the source of the stress, you will either withdraw into your own 'head space' or lash out at people. You need to find ways of constructively releasing stress and tension, as one way you try and release it is by focusing on a specific goal and working extra hard to distract yourself. This just intensifies the problem, and you will find that listening to something calming will help you better – classical or relaxing music is really beneficial for you. You will also benefit from having someone to talk through your emotions with, or who can help to distract you by doing something that focuses your mind – maybe a board game, or something like Jenga. It will help you to become more positive if you can remember something good from the past, such as reminding yourself of how well you achieved a difficult goal. Because writing is so important to you, keeping a diary of your thoughts and feelings would also help.

• Cancer

If you are Cancer, you will have times when you are just like the crab you symbolise; you will find there are often times when you need to shrink back into your shell and hide from the world – you retreat into your house. Any form of anxiety will weigh heavily on your soul, and, sometimes, you don't even try to fight it. Cancer is a sensitive sign, and you may tend to slip into a 'woe is me' complex if you're not careful. You generally find that you are naturally drawn to seclusion when you are stressed and want to spend time in your home; this can be very beneficial for your mental health and wellbeing, but it can be counter-productive if it is overused, as too much time alone can cause you to become defensive, argumentative or difficult to reason with. You need to channel your stress and introspective energy into something productive, like keeping a diary. Regular, honest conversations with yourself can be wonderfully healing and enlightening. It will also help you if you can focus your energy into methodical yet creative tasks, especially if it offers some kind of nurturing reward, like cooking. You can still do such tasks at home, alone, but, because you are focusing on the task, it will prevent you from becoming too self-absorbed. You need something to nurture to take you out of yourself – a pet, for example, or a rare and temperamental pot plant. You need to learn how to focus outward when you get stressed, not keep your emotions locked in. Taking luxurious baths is very good at helping you unwind, so try and make them part of your routine, especially if you are feeling overwhelmed.

• Leo

If you are Leo, you are very sensitive to criticism; unfortunately, your pride and ego often won't let you analyse and accept your mistakes. You need to deal with tension and stress immediately and intensely. You are likely to cry; you'll probably wait until you're alone, but tears will almost certainly flow. However, once that initial overflow of emotion has passed, you're good at putting on a brave face. You are good at putting things into perspective and will often find the humour in any situation. You may even find that you sort of enjoy being stressed, because that means you have an opportunity to impress people. You like to feel competent; you love to be admired for your capability. This drive to prove yourself can be a detriment, however, when you take on too much and refuse to admit it. Taking on too much responsibility and feeling that you have to impress others can create chronic, unresolved stress. You work well under pressure and can certainly operate at a high level in busy situations, but that won't counteract your feelings of stress. Stress, when ignored, will manifest in physical ways (crying is a one, nausea is another). You may also get more and more inward-looking when you're feeling overworked and overwhelmed. To counter this, try to reduce your obligations where you can, and be more sociable. Giving and receiving attention is good for you, as well as things like dancing or joining a group – a book club or the local dramatic society, for example. You need someone to compliment you on something and this will usually cheer you up.

• Virgo

If you are Virgo, you are somebody who likes to do things properly; you want to fix problems on your own and you don't want anybody to help. You might even get irritable if something is stressing you out and somebody tries to offer a solution. You often feel worried or guilty, or can suffer doubts about whether you are doing the right thing. You are extremely competent but can be very self-critical, and this causes you to sometimes project these feelings of disappointment onto the people around you. You may find that any stress you feel leads to digestive problems or stomach-aches. You need calm environments to balance your naturally high energy and stress levels. This may mean that you tend towards things like neutral or colour-coordinated designs and a minimalist lifestyle. Your home needs to become your happy place. You need a space that feels your own, away from your regular routine, to which you can withdraw for moments of solitude and tranquillity; this can be a space in your house – indulging in your bath with the perfect mix of essential oils, for example, or find somewhere outside, such as going to the same table at a local café or sitting on a park bench that has a nice view. Being pampered is a good way for you to release stress, so either go and have treatments somewhere or try and regularly do treatments on yourself. Also spending time nurturing yourself is beneficial for you – do your hair or make up, and this helps you to unwind. You need to try and find occasions in your day when you feel cherished as this helps you to relax

• Libra
If you are Libra, you will never go through a diffi-

cult time alone if you can help it. You really value the opinions of the people in your close inner circle; you take what others say very seriously and you'll frequently reach out to others for advice, or just to talk to them. You are not very good at dealing with high-stress situations; you value balance and harmony above everything else, so when life does not reflect those values, you can easily get stressed and tense. You need to be in pleasant, harmonious surroundings as you have such a highly developed artistic sense. You can be prone to bouts of self-pity and sometimes use the phrase, "Why me?" quite a lot. However, even though you don't like feeling stressed, you tend not to do anything to reduce it – you would much rather just wait for it to go away on its own. Instead of just waiting, though, you should try to channel your stress into coping mechanisms through creativity. Do something like painting or drawing (use your non-dominant hand and make sure to paint or draw using emotion and instinct, rather than to achieve a specific goal), or wander aimlessly through a museum (or somewhere beautiful or elegant), or listen to various styles of music. You need to use the Arts to diffuse any tension you feel. It also helps if you have someone to talk to who can encourage you out of your sorrowful mood and give practical advice, motivating you to change things in your life for the better.

● Scorpio

If you are Scorpio, you are highly sensitive, but you don't like people to know it. Therefore, you can become secretive and tend to withdraw when feeling challenged or overwhelmed. You may dislike talking to others about your anxieties or hardships, but you may also get upset when your friends don't know why you're stressed. It's important to remember that you can't have it both ways. You try to analyse your feelings of any stress or tension rather than deal with it directly. Scorpio is the most subconsciously influenced of all the signs and the protective barrier between the conscious and subconscious mind is thin; subconscious thoughts can flood into the consciousness, which can overwhelm you, causing sadness and tension. You don't tend to show your feelings and appear very composed. However, it is hard for you to acknowledge that your mind could be the reason for any stress, as you don't like to admit to weaknesses. Someone needs to talk to you, to help you change your attitude and analyse the situation from the outside. Generally, you let stress and tension build to a high level before you want to do anything about it. You need to learn to release your feelings before things build up too much – have a cry or talk to a friend – and don't feel ashamed or weak just because you are as vulnerable as everyone else. You need to work through stress and emotional turmoil by using your creativity. It is important for you to feel as though what you do is worthwhile, and you must keep busy to find outlets for your intense emotional energy. Remember, as well as the Scorpion, another symbol for Scorpio is the Eagle – you can always rise above any limitations.

• Sagittarius

If you are Sagittarius, you tend to prefer to joke about serious or stressful situations since you typically avoid emotional turmoil at all costs. You will throw yourself into everything with blind optimism and rush into things without any plan, starting with lots of enthusiasm, but this quickly progresses to burnout. However, because you are ruled by Jupiter (the lucky planet), everything often 'just works out'. But when this luck falters – which it inevitably will from time to time – you can find yourself in too deep with no strategy for how to emerge unscathed. You tend to dissipate your energy, shooting your arrows in all directions without even checking where the targets are! Then when your energy drops and you become stressed, instead of sorting through the introspective and productive tools at your disposal, you tend to seek comfort in the company of others and over-commit to social gatherings. And, since many Sagittarians want to maintain a 'cool' or likeable image, you're unlikely to open up about your stress in these circumstances. You don't like to feel you have a problem with stress.

You want to sort it out as quickly as possible and get out of the mess you are in, and, if someone can give you a push to change something, you will start acting immediately. You may often feel that you want to run away or escape when things start getting stressful, but, if you can face your issues and deal with them, you will better understand and deal with sources of stress throughout your life. You will instinctively want to do physical exercise to release stress, but it is really important that you do things that benefit your mind too. You could learn something completely new to you, such as a new language. Or do something like meditation, which will probably feel uncomfortable and boring at first, but it will help settle your restless soul. It also benefits you to laugh out loud, so have a store of things that encourage this and turn to them in times of stress.

• Capricorn

If you are Capricorn, you tend to accept stress as a fact of life. While this perspective can be useful and admirable, it can also be damaging when you fail to address the root of a persistent problem. For example, if you're in a job that routinely stresses you, you will probably just continue to work through it instead of asking yourself, "Is this really the job for me?" You are very good at handling stress; you may react anxiously and nervously at first, but you will almost always soldier on. You can work through pressure in a

very methodical way, adeptly and logically handling difficult situations. You even pride yourself
on your ability to remain grounded and self-sufficient in times of crisis. Remember, however, that
nobody can do everything alone. If you reach
out for help, chances are you'll find that you've
surrounded yourself with highly capable people.
There's no shame in a little delegation, and this
goes for emotional baggage, too. You always need
to feel in control, and you probably don't like feeling emotionally vulnerable; you could have a degree of emotional inhibition, but you need someone to talk to who can keep prompting you out of
your self-conscious state and acknowledging your
successes. The best thing to help you release your
stress and tension is physical exercise. You may
tend to neglect your physical well-being when
faced with mental challenges, feeling that if you
stop working you will feel lazy or unproductive.
However, you will find it actually has the opposite effect. It also helps if you have time to process
your reaction to exercise, as then you realise how
beneficial it is for you.

• Aquarius

If you are Aquarius, you tend to create your own
stress because you are the biggest procrastinators
in the zodiac. Aquarius is the sign most concerned
with the big picture, and you have an optimistic
'there's always tomorrow' attitude, so you may
have a hard time staying focused on what needs

to be done now. You also hate feeling cornered or trapped, and the feeling that you have a lack of options will trigger a great deal of anxiety – you don't do very well with fixed deadlines, for example. When you feel stressed or tense, you will probably withdraw or grow detached because you have difficulty with knowing how to process intense emotions. You generally prefer not to deal with stress immediately, although you want to get rid of the 'stressed' feeling as soon as possible. You tend to reach out to every single person you know for help because you like to see issues from every possible angle. However, you're very stubborn, so you'll probably do exactly what you wanted to do in the first place! Even if you did take advice from someone, you wouldn't admit it. Despite being talkative and hypothetically open about your stress, you can often feel emotionally isolated, feeling that no one truly understands what you're going through. You need to try to meet new people and get out of your comfort zone. Sometimes, advice from a relative stranger is more valuable than advice from someone who knows you and your behavioural patterns too well. You have a subconscious feeling of mind over matter so tend to push yourself too hard, so it is important that you take time to have sensible and regular eating and sleeping patterns. It also helps if you can find original outlets for your artistic talents.

• Pisces

If you are Pisces, you are very good at noticing stress and tension in your life because you tend to be very intuitive and self-aware. Instead of letting an emotion bubble up inexplicably inside of you and analysing your way through it later, you can sense the root of an emotion almost immediately, as though you can hover outside your own self and appraise your anxiety, jumping to a third-party, analytical perspective. You often cope with stress by embracing change, especially in a cliched, physical way – for example, dyeing your hair after a breakup or getting a tattoo when you feel overwhelmed. You are a bit like a psychic sponge, often confused about which feelings and emotions are actually yours and which belong to others. You tend to use fashion as a means of escapism, trying on different lifestyles and personalities to deal with being confused by your own. However, you have a good imagination and can easily distance yourself from your stress, as if it belongs to another person entirely. You can't ignore your stress forever, though, and it helps if you are in a friendly and loving circle as you need the support of friends around to comfort you and make you feel safe and needed. You will probably cry (and you often cry for others, not just yourself), and you can then come back recharged. Because you are generally the type of person who readily put others' needs ahead of your own, you must remember to prioritise genuine and lasting self-care. Make a special place in your house that has a gentle atmosphere with subdued lighting and relaxing music. Eat well, get a good night's sleep, and drink plenty of water. Remind yourself that you are at your most helpful when you're feeling healthy and refreshed. You must learn to ground yourself; it is so important that you connect with reality regularly. Saunas and spa days will also benefit you. You will do best if you can find a balance between remaining grounded and escaping reality, so something like dancing, acting or drama can help, as you can be someone else but within strict boundaries.

MINDFULNESS AS PART OF YOUR LIFE

Hopefully, reading this book has motivated you to give mindfulness a try and helped you decide what types of things you can do to bring it into your life. You don't have to do things in the order I've written! You can practise the Attention and Sensation exercises first, as they are often easier to dip in and out of. Or find something that gives you flow, as spending time doing an activity we love is so very beneficial, and you may already do a hobby anyway. If so, be aware of whether you do experience flow; if not, then why not? Are you challenged enough, for example? You may find being a fly on the wall quite hard initially, but it is worth persevering with that technique as it is such a valuable tool for managing emotions and controlling thoughts.

When we begin to practise mindfulness, we develop the ability to feel temporarily more positive or centred as a result. And when we continue to practise mindfulness, what starts out as a temporary feeling of centredness becomes increasingly more frequent. Then, when we continue with the practice, we realise that we are now operating routinely from a space of centredness rather than from a space of mind-wandering or a space of stress. This is when we will have turned the corner into really reaping the benefits of the mindfulness practice, when we're able to become mindful, regardless of what's happening to us, or outside of ourselves. And, whatever our Astrology sign, this will be the very thing that transforms our life.

REFERENCES AND FURTHER STUDY

Books and Scientific papers:

- Happiness around the world: The paradox of happy peasants and miserable millionaires. *C Graham*
- Bright-Sided. *Barbara Ehrenreich*
- The Psychology of Religion and Coping. *Kenneth Pargament*
- A wandering mind is an unhappy mind. *MA Killingsworth & DT Gilbert*
- Search Inside Yourself. *Chade Meng Tan*
- The Art and Science of Mindfulness. *Professor Shauna Shapiro*
- Mindfulness and Psychotherapy. *Sara Lazar*
- The Attention Revolution. *Alan Wallace*
- How We Know What Isn't So. *Tom Gilovich*
- 10% Happier. *Dan Harris*
- Waking Up. *Sam Harris*
- Smart Change. *Art Markman*
- The psychology of happiness. *Mihaly Csikszentmihalyi*

Astrology

For any aspect of astrology, or if you would like to know the main signs that are prominent in your chart to help with mindfulness practice then contact me via email at karenmarshastrology@gmail.com

For daily astrology updates follow my Facebook page (Karen Marsh Astrology)

Meditation CDs

For information on meditation and other spiritual practises see www.donnamaxine.com

About the Author

Karen Marsh has had a lifelong fascination with astrology, becoming a qualified astrologer, as well as obtaining degrees in teaching both people and animals. That love for teaching and astrology turned out to be just the beginning of what would be a life filled with peace, happiness, and an unending quest to help others understand and practice mindfulness that's tailored to their personality type as outlined by their astrological birth right. Her desire to help others prompted her to write a book that would outline her approach and help them lead happy lives.

When not helping people or animals, Karen enjoys being outdoors in her garden, baking, making jam, crafting, and spending time with her family, her menagerie of pets, or when she has time, reading a good book in her home in South West England.

Printed in Great Britain
by Amazon

48910110R00118